The Waite Group's
Essential Guide to
Microsoft® C

RELATED TITLES

The Waite Group's Essential Guide to ANSI C
Naba Barkakati

The Waite Group's Essential Guide to Turbo C®
Naba Barkakati

The Waite Group's C Primer Plus, Revised Edition
Mitchell Waite, Stephen Prata, and Donald Martin

The Waite Group's Advanced C Primer ++
Stephen Prata

The Waite Group's Microsoft® C Bible
Naba Barkakati

The Waite Group's QuickC™ Bible
Naba Barkakati

The Waite Group's Turbo C® Bible
Naba Barkakati

The Waite Group's Microsoft® C Programming for the PC,
Revised Edition   Robert Lafore

The Waite Group's Turbo C® Programming for the PC,
Revised Edition   Robert Lafore

The Waite Group's C++ Programming
John Berry

The Waite Group's Inside the Amiga® with C, Second Edition
John Berry

The Waite Group's MS-DOS® Bible, Third Edition *(forthcoming)*
Steven Simrin

The Waite Group's MS-DOS® Developer's Guide, Second Edition
John Angermeyer, Kevin Jaeger, et al.

The Waite Group's UNIX® Primer Plus
Mitchell Waite, Stephen Prata, and Donald Martin

The Waite Group's UNIX® System V Primer, Revised Edition
Mitchell Waite, Stephen Prata, and Donald Martin

The Waite Group's UNIX® System V Bible
Stephen Prata and Donald Martin

*For the retailer nearest you, or to order directly from the publisher,
call 800-428-SAMS. In Indiana, Alaska, and Hawaii call 317-298-5699.*

The Waite Group's
Essential Guide to
Microsoft® C

Nabajyoti Barkakati

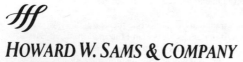

HOWARD W. SAMS & COMPANY

A Division of Macmillan, Inc.
4300 West 62nd Street
Indianapolis, Indiana 46268 USA

FIRST EDITION
FIRST PRINTING—1989

International Standard Book Number: 0-672-22674-X
Library of Congress Catalog Card Number: 89-60250

From The Waite Group, Inc.
Development Editor: *Mitchell Waite*
Editorial Editor: *James Stockford*
Managing Editor: *Scott Calamar*

From Howard W. Sams & Company
Acquisitions Editor: *Richard K. Swadley*
Development Editor: *James Rounds*
Manuscript Editor: *Sara Bernhardt Black*
Production Coordinator: *Marjorie Hopper*
Designer: *Glenn Santner*
Illustrator: *T.R. Emrick*
Cover Artist: *Kevin Caddell*
Indexer: *Ted Laux*
Compositor: *Shepard Poorman Communications Corp.*

Printed in the United States of America

Trademark Acknowledgments

Contents

Preface

C is rapidly becoming the language of choice for developing PC applications. A primary reason for this C revolution is the availability of high-quality optimizing compilers such as Microsoft C 5.1, which is a full-featured C compiler, with a high degree of compliance to the proposed draft ANSI standard for C, a huge library with nearly 370 routines including graphics, and the full-screen CodeView debugger.

Much of Microsoft C's power remains untapped, however. There are so many routines in the library that often you may not know whether a routine exists to suit your need. What is missing from the Microsoft C 5.1 product is a handy guide that lets you locate what you need, when you need it.

This conveniently sized book is meant to be a reference guide to Microsoft C 5.1 for intermediate to professional level programmers. It is designed to give you instant access to most of the commonly used routines in the Microsoft C 5.1 library. It features:

► An overview of the C language keywords including the new ANSI standard features,
► A summary of the features specific to Microsoft C 5.1 including a description of the compiler and linker options,
► Individual reference entries for the library routines, and
► A comprehensive index to help you look up topics and functions.

This book is not an introduction to C nor is it a comprehensive reference manual for Microsoft C 5.1; refer to the further reading list in the next section for introductory and advanced books on C. In particular, you should consult *The Waite Group's Microsoft C Bible* for more details on the Microsoft C 5.1 library routines. Here we assume that you are already familiar with C and want to get an overview of Microsoft C 5.1 and its library. Even if you are already familiar with Microsoft C, this guide can serve as ready reference for the keywords and the library functions.

Acknowledgments

I would like to thank Mitch Waite for giving me the opportunity to work on this book and Scott Calamar for providing the support necessary to complete the book on time. Most of all, I thank my wife Leha and my daughters Ivy and Emily for their love and support. It is to them that I dedicate this book and all others to come.

Nabajyoti Barkakati

How to Use This
Essential Guide

Organization

The Waite Group's Essential Guide to Microsoft C is organized in
five parts. Part I is an overview of the Microsoft C language and
the Microsoft C compiler. Here you will find information on specific features of the C language, such as *volatile* and *const*, new
types such as *enum* and *void*, and the new *token-pasting* and
string-izing operators of the preprocessor. A summary description of the Microsoft C compiler and linker is also provided here.
Parts II through V cover the Microsoft C library. Each group of
library functions starts with a short introduction followed by al-
phabetically arranged reference entries on the functions in that
group. Each reference entry is presented in the standard form
shown in Figure I-1.

Part II describes the dynamic memory allocation facilities in
C and explains how to handle abnormal conditions occurring
during the execution of your program. This part presents routines such as *malloc* and *free* and explains how advanced process control routines such as *setjmp* and *longjmp* work. Buffer
manipulation routines such as *memmove* and *memcmp* are also
presented here. Part III goes on to the data processing aspects of
the C library: how to compute math formulas, manipulate
strings, search and sort, and get the current time and date. Part
IV describes the file I/O and DOS/BIOS support routines in the
Microsoft C library. Here you will find a discussion of the
"stream" model of files in C, how I/O is performed with the
streams, and how you can access the services offered by the
BIOS and MS-DOS. Finally, Part V presents the Microsoft C
graphics library, which supports a variety of PC display adapters
including CGA, EGA, VGA, and the Hercules Graphics Card.
The graphics library contains all the tools necessary to build a
full graphics-based application, including the capability to draw
basic shapes, control colors, and manipulate text in several different fonts.

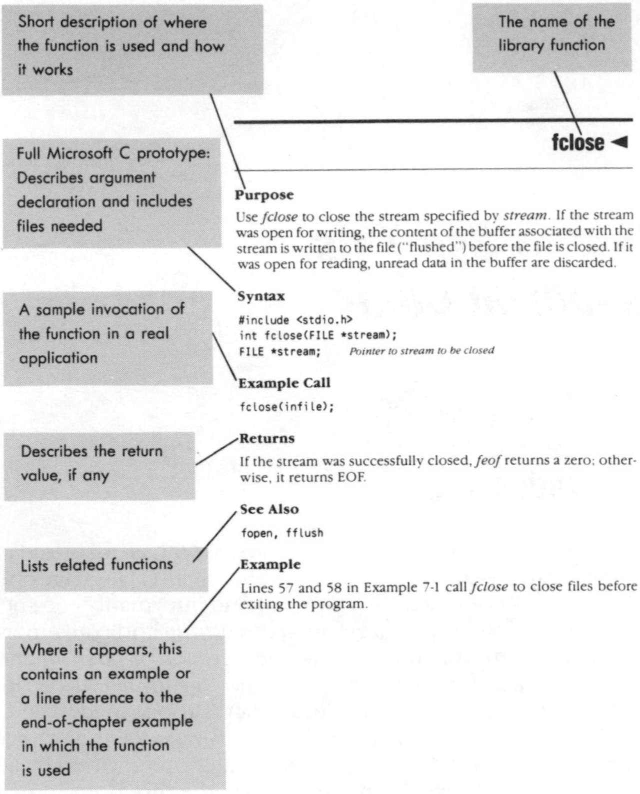

Short description of where the function is used and how it works

The name of the library function

fclose ◄

Full Microsoft C prototype: Describes argument declaration and includes files needed

Purpose

Use *fclose* to close the stream specified by *stream*. If the stream was open for writing, the content of the buffer associated with the stream is written to the file ("flushed") before the file is closed. If it was open for reading, unread data in the buffer are discarded.

Syntax

A sample invocation of the function in a real application

```
#include <stdio.h>
int fclose(FILE *stream);
FILE *stream;      Pointer to stream to be closed
```

Example Call

```
fclose(infile);
```

Describes the return value, if any

Returns

If the stream was successfully closed, *feof* returns a zero; otherwise, it returns EOF.

See Also

```
fopen, fflush
```

Lists related functions

Example

Lines 57 and 58 in Example 7-1 call *fclose* to close files before exiting the program.

Where it appears, this contains an example or a line reference to the end-of-chapter example in which the function is used

Figure I-1. Reference Entry Format

What You Need to Know to Use This Guide

This guide assumes that you are already familiar with C, but it does not require you to be knowledgeable about the specific features of Microsoft C and its library. The goal of this book is to provide a handy, concise, and practical guide to the most essential aspects of the Microsoft C language and the library routines.

If you are beginning to learn C and want to start with an awareness of all ANSI features, the latest book by Kernighan and Ritchie[1] will be a good place to start. Until the ANSI standard C came out, the previous edition of their book[2] served as the de facto standard because Ritchie was the developer of C. This original edition of the book is often referred to as the "K&R standard." If you need a reference guide for the ANSI C language and the standard library, you will find *The Waite Group's Essential Guide to ANSI C*[3] handy. This book provides the latest details on the keywords and routines specified by the ANSI X3J11 committee. For learning C using Microsoft C on the IBM PC, you can use Lafore's book[4] as a starting place. Another alternative is the best-selling introduction to the C language by Waite, Prata, and Martin[5]; it is based on UNIX C. You can follow up with the more advanced guide by Prata[6].

The Waite Group's Microsoft C Bible[7] is ideal as a comprehensive tutorial and reference book on Microsoft C 5.1. That book complements this essential guide by providing further compiler-specific details, descriptions of all functions in the Microsoft C library, extensive tutorials, and complete example programs.

Reference List

1. Brian W. Kernighan and Dennis M. Ritchie, *The C Programming Language*, Second Edition, Prentice-Hall, Inc., Englewood Cliffs, NJ, 1988, 261 pages.

2. Brian W. Kernighan and Dennis M. Ritchie, *The C Programming Language*, First Edition, Prentice-Hall, Inc., Englewood Cliffs, NJ, 1978, 228 pages.

3. Nabajyoti Barkakati, *The Waite Group's Essential Guide to ANSI C*, Howard W. Sams & Company, Indianapolis, IN, 1988, 248 pages.

4. Robert Lafore, *The Waite Group's, Microsoft C Programming for the PC*, Howard W. Sams & Company, Indianapolis, IN, 1989, 776 pages.

5. Mitchell Waite, Stephen Prata, and Donald Martin, *The Waite Group's C Primer Plus*, Revised Edition, Howard W. Sams & Company, Indianapolis, IN, 1987, 576 pages.

6. Stephen Prata, *Advanced C Primer++*, Howard W. Sams & Company, Indianapolis, IN, 1986, 512 pages.

7. Nabajyoti Barkakati, *The Waite Group's Microsoft C Bible*, Howard W. Sams & Company, Indianapolis, IN, 1988, 808 pages.

Typographic Conventions

The Waite Group's Essential Guide to Microsoft C uses a simple notational style. All function names, keywords, and variable names appearing in text are typeset in *italics*. Annotation of variables under the syntax headings in the reference pages is also italicized. File names and constants are in uppercase roman. All program listings are typeset in a monospace font for easy reading.

Every effort has been made to reproduce single computer lines in their entirety. The practical limits of typeset line length, however, cause an occasional line break. Where this occurs, the broken portion is placed at the right margin of the second line as a visual signal.

I

The C Language and Microsoft C

1

Overview of the Microsoft C Language

Introduction

Many C compilers are available for use with PCs. Microsoft C offers one of the best environments for program development with such utilities as MAKE for automating recompilations and with the CodeView symbolic debugger with full-screen user interface. Version 5.0, introduced in 1987, improves an already good product. The compiler now conforms to most aspects of the proposed ANSI standard for C, and the library has been enhanced with many more routines, most notably for system calls (for accessing DOS and BIOS services) and for graphics. The QuickC integrated programming environment provides new ease of use. In 1988 a new version, Microsoft C 5.1 was introduced. This update provides support for the OS/2 operating system. With it, you can build both OS/2 "protected" mode and "real" mode (which is the same as MS-DOS) applications.

This essential guide is designed as a handy reference for Microsoft C and its library. The focus is on the keywords of the language, the preprocessor directives, and the library routines. This chapter is a quick summary of the Microsoft C keywords and operators. Chapter 2 summarizes the features of the Microsoft C 5.1 compiler and linker that you can use to build your programs.

Structure of a C Program

As shown in Figure 1-1, a file containing a C program consists of preprocessor directives, declarations of variables and functions, a *main* function, the body of the main function, and other functions. The body of each function, including *main*, contains expressions and statements.

The "preprocessor" is a facility unique to C. As its name implies, it processes the source file before the compilation begins.

3

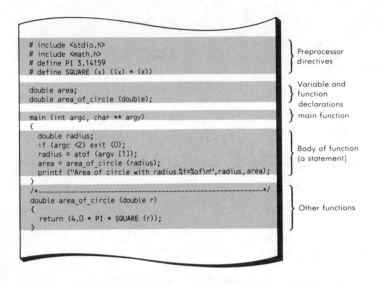

Figure 1-1. Structure of a C Program

The preprocessor performs several important tasks such as incorporating the contents of another file into the C program (the *#include* directive) and replacing one string pattern in the program with another (the *#define* directive).

"Declarations" state which variables and functions will be used in the program and what type of data will be used by each. Declarations outside the body of the functions are "global," that is, they are available to any functions, including code in other source files. Variables and functions from other files used by functions in this file are also declared: These declarations are *external*. Variables "local" to a function are declared within the body of the function. Declaring a variable also informs the compiler to allocate storage for that variable. Storage is not allocated, however, for variables being referenced from other files.

The "body of a function" contains declarations that are local to that function and statements and expressions that implement the procedure being performed by that function. The "statements" control the flow of execution and use the values provided by expressions. An "expression" is a combination of operators, variables, and function calls that result in a single value. An expression is always part of a statement.

Preprocessor Directives

The preprocessor provides three important services that enable users to make their programs modular, more easily readable, and easier to customize for different computer systems: including the contents of a file into a C program (file inclusion), replacing one string with another (token replacement and macro processing), and compiling selected portions of a program (conditional compilation). Table 1-1 summarizes the preprocessor directives in Microsoft C.

Table 1-1. Microsoft C Preprocessor Directives

Directive	Meaning
# operator	String-izing operator
Example:	#define show(x) printf(#x)
	show(me); expands to *printf("me");*
## operator	Token-pasting operator
Example:	#define version(x) MSC##x
	version(5) results in the token *MSC5*
#define	Define a symbol or a macro (you can redefine a macro with the same expression as often as you want)
Example:	#define twice(x) ((x) + (x))
	r = twice(2.0); sets *r* to *4.0*
#elif	Else if operator (see example for *#if*)
#else	Else operator (see example for *#if*)
#endif	Mark the end of an *#if* directive
#error	Produce diagnostic message
Example:	#ifdef NO_EXT_KEYS
	#error Please recompile with the /Ze option.
	#endif
#if	Conditional directive
Example:	#if !defined(FILE_1_INCLUDED)
	#include ⟨file1.h⟩
	#elif defined(INCLUDE_FILE_2)
	#include ⟨file2.h⟩
	#else
	#include ⟨file3.h⟩
	#endif
#ifdef	Equivalent to *#if defined*
#ifndef	Equivalent to *#if !defined*
#include	File inclusion
Example:	#include ⟨stdio.h⟩
#line	Set the current line number
#pragma	Instruct the compiler. Microsoft C 5.1 understands a large number of #pragmas. See *The Waite Group's Microsoft C Bible* for a complete list.
#undef	Remove the definition of a symbol

The Microsoft C compiler includes a number of preprocessor symbols that are predefined. Table 1-2 lists these macros. Note that the proposed ANSI C standard stipulates that all such predefined macros must start with a leading underscore (_) followed by a capital letter or another underscore. You cannot use *#undef* to remove the definitions of these macros.

Table 1-2. Predefined Macros in Microsoft C

Macro Name	Defined to Be
_CHAR_UNSIGNED	This symbol is defined when the /J option is used. This definition changes the default type of char variables from signed to unsigned.
_ _DATE_ _	The date of translation of the source file in the form of a string of the form "MMM DD YYYY" (such as "Oct 16 1988").
_ _FILE_ _	A string containing the name of the source file.
_ _LINE_ _	The line number of the current source file as a decimal constant.
MSDOS	This symbol indicates that the operating system is MS-DOS.
M_I86	This symbol identifies the machine for which the compiler generates code as a member of the Intel 80x86 family.
M_I86xM	This symbol identifies the memory model. The letter x will depend on the memory model. In the small model, the symbol is M_I86SM, in the compact model M_I86CM, in the medium model M_I86MM, and in the large model M_I86LM. In the huge model, two symbols are defined: M_I86LM and M_I86HM.
NO_EXT_KEYS	This symbol becomes defined when the /Za option is used to disable all extensions specific to Microsoft C (also see _ _STDC_ _).
_ _STDC_ _	This symbol is defined as 1 when you compile with the /Za flag, which checks your source code for strict ANSI compatibility.
_ _TIME_ _	This is the time that the preprocessor began processing the current source file. This is a string of the form: "HH:MM:SS" (for example, "15:32:10").
_ _TIMESTAMP_ _	Defined as a string containing the date and time of last modification to the file, expressed in the form "DDD MMM DD HH:MM:SS YYYY". Here is an example: "Mon Oct 10 19:35:52 1988".

Function Prototypes

Function prototypes is probably the most publicized feature of ANSI C. It requires you to declare the formal parameters that a function takes as well as the return value. If a function *locate_* *char* that returns a pointer to a *char* takes a string and an integer as an argument, the ANSI-style prototype for this function will be

```
char *locate_char(char *, int);
```

with the formal argument list shown with the type of each parameter only. You may include an identifier for each formal parameter, such as

```
char *locate_char(char *str, int c);
```

In this case, the prototype can look exactly like the first line in the definition of the function, except that in the prototype you terminate the line with a semicolon.

C Operators

Table 1-3 summarizes the operators available in C. Each operator is shown with an example and a short explanation of its usage.

Table 1-3. Operators in C

Operator	Name	Example	Explanation
Arithmetic Operators			
*	Multiplication	x*y	Multiply x and y
/	Division	x/y	Divide x by y
%	Modulo	x%y	Remainder of x divided by y
+	Addition	x+y	Add x and y
−	Subtraction	x−y	Subtract y from x
++	Increment	x++	Increment x after use
−−	Decrement	−−x	Decrement x before use
−	Negation	−x	Negate the value of x
+	Unary Plus	+x	Value of x (new in ANSI C)
Relational and Logical Operators			
>	Greater than	x>y	1 if x exceeds y, else 0
>=	Greater than or equal to	x>=y	1 if x is greater than or equal to y, else 0
<	Less than	x>y	1 if y exceeds x, else 0
<=	Less than or equal to	x<=y	1 if x is less than or equal to y, else 0
==	Equal to	x==y	1 if x equals y, else 0
!=	Not equal to	x!==y	1 if x and y unequal, else 0
!	Logical NOT	!x	1 if x is 0, else 0

Table 1-3. (cont.)

Operator	Name	Example	Explanation
&&	Logical AND	x&&y	0 if either x or y is 0
||	Logical OR	x||y	0 if both x and y are 0

Assignment Operators

=	Assignment	x = y;	Put value of y into x
O=	Compound assignment	x O= y;	Equivalent to x = x O y; where O is one of the operators: + − * / % ⟨⟨ ⟩⟩ & ^ |

Data Access and Size Operators

[ ]	Array element	x[0]	First element of array x
.	Member selection	s.x	Member x in structure s
→	Member selection	p→x	Member named x in a structure that p points to
*	Indirection	*p	Contents of location whose address is in p
&	Address of	&x	Address of x
sizeof	Size in bytes	sizeof(x)	Size of x in bytes

Bitwise Operators

~	Bitwise complement	~x	Flip 1 bits to 0 and 0 bits to 1
&	Bitwise AND	x&y	Bitwise AND of x and y
|	Bitwise OR	x|y	Bitwise OR of x and y
^	Bitwise exclusive OR	x^y	Value with 1's at bits where corresponding bits of x and y differ
⟨⟨	Left shift	x ⟨⟨ 4	x shifted to the left by 4-bit positions
⟩⟩	Right shift	x ⟩⟩ 4	x shifted to the right by 4-bit positions

Miscellaneous Operators

( )	Function	malloc(10)	Call malloc with argument 10
(type)	Type cast	(double)i	i converted to a double
? :	Conditional	x1 ? x2 : x3	If x1 is not 0, x2 is evaluated, else x3 is evaluated
,	Sequential evaluation	i+ +, j+ +	First increment i, then increment j

Operator Precedence

Typically, you will use several operands and operators in many statements of your program. For example, if you write

```
*ptr[2]
```

will the result be the value to which ptr[2] points or is it the third element from the location whose address is in *ptr*? To determine this, you need to know the order in which operators are applied. This is specified by the operator's "precedence" in C, which is summarized in Table 1-4. Operators with highest precedence—those that are applied first—are shown first. The order in which operators at the same level get evaluated (associativity) is also shown. If you consult the table, you will find that the [ ] operators have precedence over the * operator. So in our example, ptr[2] will be evaluated first and then the "indirection" operator applied, resulting in the value whose address is in ptr [2].

Table 1-4. Operator Precedence and Associativity in C

Operator Type	Operators	Associativity
Expression	( ) [ ] . →	Left to right
Unary	− + ~ ! * & + + − − sizeof (type)	Right to left
Multiplicative	* / %	Left to right
Additive	+ −	Left to right
Shift	⟨⟨ ⟩⟩	Left to right
Relational (inequality)	⟨ ⟨ = ⟩ ⟩ =	Left to right
Relational (equality)	= = ! =	Left to right
Bitwise AND	&	Left to right
Bitwise XOR	^	Left to right
Bitwise OR	|	Left to right
Logical AND	&&	Left to right
Logical OR	||	Left to right
Conditional	? :	Right to left
Assignment	= * = / = % = + = − = ⟨⟨ = ⟩⟩ = & = | = ^ =	Right to left
Sequential evaluation	,	Left to right

Microsoft C Keywords

Finally, Table 1-5 lists all of the keywords of Microsoft C. Individual reference entries for the keywords follow.

Table 1-5. Microsoft C Keywords

auto	case	char	continue
break	cdecl	const	default

Table 1-5. (cont.)

do	fortran	pascal	switch
double	goto	register	typedef
else	huge	return	union
enum	if	_saveregs	unsigned
_export	int	short	void
extern	interrupt	signed	volatile
far	_loadds	sizeof	while
float	long	static	
for	near	struct	

► auto

Purpose

Use the *auto* storage class specifier to declare temporary variables. These variables are created upon entering a block statement and destoyed upon exiting it. Local variables of a function have the *auto* storage class by default.

Example

In the following example, the variables *i*, *limit*, and *sum* are created only when the *if* statement is true—when the user presses a *C*.

```
#include <stdio.h>
main()
{
    int c;
    c = getchar();
    if(c == 'C')
    {
        auto int i, limit, sum;
        printf("Sum from 1 to ?");
        scanf(" %d",&limit);
/* Compute sum from 1 to limit */
        for(i=0, sum=0; i <= limit; sum += i, i++);
        printf("\nSum  from 1 to %d = %d\n", limit, sum);
    }
}
```

See Also

extern, register, static

auto

break ◀

Purpose

Use *break* to exit the innermost *do*, *while*, or *for* loop. Also use it to exit from a *switch* statement.

Example

The following code fragment adds the numbers from 1 to 10 in an endless loop. It uses *break* to exit the loop.

```
sum = 0;
i = 0;
while(1)
{
    sum += i;
    i++;
    if(i > 10) break;
}
```

See Also

case, do, for, switch, while

case ◀

Purpose

Use *case* to label cases in a *switch* statement.

Example

See *switch* for an example.

See Also

default, switch

cdecl ◀

Purpose

Use this keyword to force the C argument passing convention for a function when the rest of the program is compiled with the /Gc option, which enables the Pascal calling convention.

Example

```
double cdecl findmax(int numpoints, double *datapoints);
```

See Also

fortran, pascal

---

 char

Purpose

Use *char* to declare character variables and arrays.

Example

The following example declares a character, a pointer to a *char*, and an array of characters.

char c, *p_c, string[80];

See Also

double, float, int, long, short, signed, unsigned

► **const**

Purpose

Use the *const*-type qualifier to indicate that the variable that follows may not be modified by the program. This means that you cannot assign a value to that variable, increment it, or decrement it.

Example

The following example declares that the value of *x*, contents of the location whose address is *p_i*, and the pointer *p_c_i* must not be changed by the program's code.

```
const short x;      /* x is constant            */
const int *p_i;     /* *p_i is constant         */
int *const p_c_i;   /* pointer p_c_i is constant */
```

See Also

volatile

► **continue**

Purpose

Use *continue* to skip execution of a loop. It is equivalent to executing a *goto* to the end of the loop. The *continue* statement affects the innermost loop in which it appears.

continue

Example

The following *for* loop will be skipped when *i* is 5, giving us the sum of the numbers from 1 to 10, excluding 5.

```
for(i=0, sum=0; i <= 10, i++)
{
    if(i == 5) continue;
    sum += i;
}
```

See Also

```
for, if, while
```

---

default

Purpose

Use *default* as the label in a *switch* statement to mark code that will be executed when none of the *case* labels match the *switch* expression.

Example

See *switch* for an example.

See Also

```
case, switch
```

---

do

Purpose

Use *do* with *while* to form iterative loops of the kind

```
do statement while(expression);
```

where the statement is executed until the expression evaluates to 0. The expression is evaluated after each execution of the statement.

Example

The following *do* loop continues until *i* exceeds 10.

```
do
{
    sum += i;
    i++;
}
while(i >= 10);
```

do

See Also

for, if, while

► double

Purpose

Use *double* to declare double precision floating-point variables and arrays.

Example

The example declares a *double*, a pointer to a *double*, and an array of *double*s.

```
double d, *p_d, dvars[80];
```

See Also

char, float, int, long, short, signed, unsigned

► else

Purpose

Use *else* with *if* to control the flow of execution by a construct of the form

```
if (expression) statement_1 else statement_2
```

where *statement_1* is executed if the *expression* is not equal to 0; otherwise, *statement_2* is executed.

Example

See *if* for an example.

See Also

if

► enum

Purpose

Use *enum* to define an integral data type that can take its values from a list of enumerated constants. The declaration is of the form

enum

```
enum identifier { enumerated_list };
enum identifier var1, var2;
```

where the first line shows the definition of an *enum* type named *identifier* and the second line actually declares two variables *var1*, *var2* of type *identifier*. The example shows the form of the *enumerated_list* in the definition of an *enum* type.

Example

The code below makes *traffic_signal* the name of an enumerated type and declares *signal_1* as a variable of that type and *p_signal* as a pointer to *traffic_signal*. As you can see, the definition of the *enum* also allows you to initialize the entries in the enumerated list.

```
enum traffic_signal {red = 10, yellow = 20, green = 30};
enum traffic_signal signal_1, *p siqnal;
```

See Also

typedef

_export ◄

Purpose

Use the *_export* keyword, introduced in Microsoft C 5.1, for creating functions that will reside in OS/2's dynamic-link libraries (see Gordon Letwin's *Inside OS/2*, Microsoft Press, 1988, for a discussion of dynamic-link libraries and other major features of OS/2).

See Also

_loadds, _saveregs

---

extern ◄

Purpose

Use *extern* to tell the compiler that a variable or a function is defined in another module (a separate file) and that you want to use it in the current module. The data item or function must be declared in one of the program modules without the *static* or the *extern* qualifier.

Example

In the example below, the variables *current_state* and *state_table* are shared between FILE 1 and FILE 2. They are defined in FILE 1 and declared to be *extern* in FILE 2.

```
/* F I L E    1 */
int current_state, state_table[MAXSTATE][MAXSYMB];
extern void next_state(int in_symbol);
main()
{
  int in_symbol;
  :
  current_state = 0;
  next_state(in_symbol);
  :
}

/* F I L E    2 */
void next_state(int in_symbol)
{
   extern int current_state, state_table[MAXSTATE][MAXSYMB];
   if ( current_state == 0 ) ...
   :
   current_state = state_table[current_state][in_symbol];
   :
}
```

See Also

static

► far

Purpose

Use the *far* keyword to tell the compiler to use full segment:offset address for a pointer.

Example

```
char far *buf;
```

See Also

huge, near

► float

Purpose

Use *float* to declare single precision floating-point variables and arrays.

float

Example

The example declares a *float*, a pointer to a *float*, and an array of *floats*.

```
float f, *p_f, fvars[100];
```

See Also

```
char, double, int, long, short, signed, unsigned
```

for ◀

Purpose

Use *for* to form iterative loops of the type

```
for (expression_1; expression_2; expression_3) statement
```

where the *expression_1* is evaluated once at the beginning of the loop, and the *statement* is executed until *expression_2* evaluates to 0. The third expression, *expression_3*, is evaluated after each execution of *statement*.

Example

The following *for* loop adds the numbers from 1 to *limit*, all inside the third expression in the *for* loop.

```
    :
    for(i=0, sum=0; i <= limit; sum += i, i++);
    printf("\nSum from 1 to %d = %d\n", limit, sum);
```

See Also

```
break, continue, if, switch
```

fortran ◀

Purpose

Use this keyword to declare FORTRAN-compatible data items and functions.

Example

```
char fortran string[MAXSIZE];
```

See Also

```
cdecl, pascal
```

▶ goto

Purpose

Use *goto* to jump unconditionally to a label in the current function.

Example

```
if (system_price > 6000.0) goto TooExpensive;
    :
TooExpensive:
    seek_alternative();
```

▶ huge

Purpose

Use this keyword to qualify a pointer so that the compiler maintains it in a normalized form derived by using the high-order 16 bits of the 20-bit physical address as the segment address. This ensures that pointer arithmetic will work properly even when the address differences exceed 64K.

Example

```
double huge *raw_data;
```

See Also

far, near

▶ if

Purpose

Use *if* to excute code only when certain conditions hold good. You can use *if* alone or with *else* to form constructs such as

```
if ( expression )  statement
```

or

```
if ( expression ) statement_1 else statement_2
```

where the statement following the *if* is executed if the *expression* is unequal to 0. When an *else* is present, *statement_2* is executed if *expression* is equal to 0.

if

Example

The example shows the use of *if* and *else* to pick the smaller of two variables.

```
:
if ( x <= y)  smaller = x;
else smaller = y;
:
```

See Also

else

int

Purpose

Use *int* to declare integer variables and arrays. The size qualifiers *short* and *long* should be used to declare an integer of desired size. The size of an *int* is implementation-dependent. It is guaranteed to be larger than a *short*, however.

Example

int i, x[100];

See Also

char, double, float, long, short, signed, unsigned

interrupt

Purpose

Use *interrupt* to qualify a function as an interrupt handler. When the compiler translates a function with the *interrupt* attribute, it generates code to push the registers AX, CX, DX, BX, BP, SP, SI, DI, DS, and ES (IP, CS, and the flags are pushed automatically when an interrupt handler is called). Then it sets up the DS register to point to the data segment of that function. After this initial sequence comes the code of the function. Finally, the compiler uses an IRET instruction instead of a normal RET to return from the function.

Example

```
void (interrupt far *oldint28_handler)();
:
oldint28_handler = _dos_getvect(0x28);
```

▶ __loadds

Purpose

The *__loadds* keyword, introduced in Microsoft C 5.1, causes the compiler to generate code to load the data segment register (DS) with a specific value upon entry to the function. The *data_seg* pragma specifies the segment value loaded into DS. If there are no *data_seg* pragmas in the program, the segment value set by the /ND option is used. When none of these sources for the segment value are present, the default group DGROUP is used to derive the segment value. Note that the *__loadds* function modifier has the same effect as the /Au compiler option.

Example

The following code declares *myfunction* as a function that loads the segment value MYSEG into the DS register upon entry.

```
#pragma data_seg(MYSEG)
void far _loadds myfunction(int command);
```

See Also

_export, _saveregs

▶ long

Purpose

Use *long* as a size qualifier for *int* and *unsigned int* variables. Note that *long* alone means *signed long int*. A *long* qualifier indicates that the integer data type is 4 bytes in size.

Example

The example shows the declaration of a *long int* and an *unsigned long int*.

```
long filepos;
unsigned long timer_tick;
```

See Also

char, double, float, int, short, signed, unsigned

long

near

Purpose

You can use the *near* keyword in a large model program to force the use of offset addresses only for a pointer.

Example

```
char near *a_string;
```

See Also

far, huge

pascal

Purpose

Use *pascal* to generate code using the Pascal calling convention for a function that produces more compact code than the C calling convention.

Example

```
double pascal average(int numpoints, double *data);
```

See Also

cdecl

register

Purpose

Use *register* as a storage classifier for integer data types to inform the compiler that the access to that data object should be as fast as possible. At its discretion, the compiler may use a CPU register to store that variable.

Example

```
register int i;
```

See Also

auto, extern, static

▶ return

Purpose

Use *return* to terminate execution of the current function and return control to the caller. If the function returns a value, use the statement *return ⟨expression⟩* to return the value represented by the ⟨expression⟩.

Example

The following function returns the maximum of two integers.

```
int findmax(int a, int b)
{
    if(a >= b)
        return a;
    else
        return b;
}
```

See Also

break, continue, goto

▶ __saveregs

Purpose

The *__saveregs* keyword, introduced in Microsoft C 5.1, instructs the compiler to generate code to save all CPU registers upon entering the function and restore them when exiting it. The AX register is not restored if the function returns a value.

See Also

_export, _loadds

▶ short

Purpose

Use *short* as a size qualifier for *int* and *unsigned int* variables. Note that *short* alone means *signed short int*. A *short* qualifier indicates that the integer data type is 2 bytes in size.

short

Example

The following example shows the declaration of a *short int* and an *unsigned short int*.

```
short offset;
unsigned short array_index;
```

See Also

```
char, double, float, int, long, signed, unsigned
```

---

signed ◄

Purpose

Use the *signed* qualifier to indicate that data stored in an integral type (*int*, *char*) is signed. For example, a *signed char* can take values between −128 to +127, whereas an *unsigned char* can hold values from 0 to 255. The *int* and *char* types are *signed* by default.

Example

```
int i;  /* signed by default */
signed long int x;
```

See Also

```
char, double, float, int, long, short, unsigned
```

---

sizeof ◄

Purpose

Use the *sizeof* operator to get the size of a data element in bytes. For example, you can use it to determine the size of a structure so that you can call *calloc* to allocate an array of them. Another use of *sizeof* is to compute the number of elements in an array.

Example

The following code fragment uses *sizeof* to get the size of a structure and use it as an argument to *calloc*. It also uses *sizeof* to initialize the count of elements in an array.

```
struct mytype
{
    char firstname[20];
    char lastname[20];
};
```

```
short offsets[] = {-1, 10, 20, 32, 48};
short n_offsets = sizeof(offsets)/sizeof(offsets[0]);
:
p_mytype = (struct mytype*)
calloc(100, sizeof(struct mytype));
```

See Also

typedef

static

Purpose

Use *static* to localize the declaration of a data item or a function to a program module (file). You can use this to "hide" functions and data from other modules. Static variables have permanent storage; they retain their values throughout the life of the program.

Example

In the following example, each file has its own copy of the variable *current_index*. Each copy is initialized once, and each retains its last-stored value throughout the execution of the program.

```
/*F I L E    1 */
static int current_index = 0;
main()
{
   :
   current_index = 1;
   :
}
/*F I L E    2 */
static int current_index = 0;
void some_function(void)
{
   if ( current_index == 0 ) ...
   :
   current_index = 2;
   :
}
```

See Also

auto, extern

static

struct ◄

Purpose

Use *struct* to group related data items together and give it a name by which you can refer to it later. The general form is

```
struct structure_name
{
    type item_1;
    type item_2;
    :
};
struct structure_name struct_1, struct_2;
```

where the first declaration defines a structure with a name *structure_name* and the second one declares two structures *struct_1* and *struct_2*.

Example

The following example defines a structure to be used in a linked list. It contains several members including one that is a pointer to itself.

```
struct node
{
    int node_type;
    char node_name[16];
    struct node *next;
};
struct node *p_node, first_node;
```

See Also

union

switch ◄

Purpose

Use the *switch* statement to perform a multiway branch depending on the value of an expression. The syntax is:

```
switch (expression) statement
```

Use *case* labels inside the statement to indicate what to do for each expected value of the expression. Use *break* to separate the code of one *case* label from another. A *default* label marks code to be executed if none of the *case* labels match the expression.

Example

The *switch* statement in the following example executes different routines depending on the value of *command*. Note the use
of *break* statements to keep the execution from falling through
one *case* label to another.

```
switch (command)
{
    case 'Q': exit(0);
    case 'C': connect();
              break;
    case 'S': sendfile();
              break;
    case 'P': newparams();
              break;
    case '?': showparams();
              break;
    case 'H': printf(helplist);
              break;
    default:  printf("Unknown command!\n");
}
```

See Also

```
break, case, default
```

▶ typedef

Purpose

Use *typedef* to give a new name to an existing data type. The syntax is

```
typedef existing_type new_name;
```

For example, *typedef int (*P_FUNC)( );* will allow you to use
P_FUNC as a data type that means "pointer to a function returning an integer." You can use *typedef* to build up complex declarations easily.

Example

```
typedef struct NODE
{
    struct NODE *left;
    struct NODE *right;
    char        *entry;
} NODE;
NODE topnode;  /* Declare the root node */
```

typedef

See Also

enum

union ◀

Purpose

Use *union* to allocate storage for several data items at the same location. The declaration of *union* is identical to that of *struct*, except that in a *union* all data items in the declaration share the same storage location.

Example

The example declares a *union* that stores a *short* in the same location as an array of two characters. Each individual byte of the *short* stored in the *union x* can be accessed by *x.bytes[0]* and *x.bytes[1]*.

```
union short_u
{
    short sh_val;
    char  bytes[2];
};
union short_u x;
```

See Also

struct

unsigned ◀

Purpose

Use the *unsigned* qualifier with integer data types (*char*, *int*, *short int*, and *long int*) to tell the compiler that the variable will be used to store nonnegative values only. This effectively doubles the maximum value that can be stored in that variable. Another useful feature is that arithmetic involving *unsigned* integers can never overflow because all operations are performed modulo a number that is one greater than the largest value that can be represented by that unsigned type.

Example

Here are some declarations of *unsigned* variables.

```
unsigned char data[1000];
unsigned long file_pos;
```

```
unsigned i;    /* equivalent to unsigned int i */
```

See Also

char, double, float, int, long, short, unsigned

► void

Purpose

Use the data type *void* to indicate the nonexistence of a return value or arguments in a function definition and prototype. You can use *void* * to declare a pointer to any type of data object.

Example

```
void a_function(void *buffer);
int get_something(void);
extern void *p_buf;
```

See Also

char, int, double, float

► volatile

Purpose

Use a *volatile*-type qualifier to inform the compiler that the variable that follows may be modified by factors outside the control of your program. For example, the contents of a register in the real-time clock in your system will be such a variable. The *volatile* qualifier warns the compiler that actions performed on *volatile* data must not be "optimized out." You can use the qualifier *const* together with *volatile* to qualify objects that must not be changed by your program, yet that may change due to external factors.

Example

The following code shows the declaration of the register in a real-time clock. It says that our code cannot change the contents (*p_rt_clock*), but the contents may change by itself. We are, however, free to modify the pointer *p_rt_clock* to point to another *long int*.

```
const volatile long *p_rt_clock = CLOCK_ADDRESS;
```

See Also

const

while ◄

Purpose

Use the *while* statement to construct loops such as

```
while (expression) statement
```

where the statement is executed until *expression* evaluates to 0. The *expression* is evaluated after each execution of the statement.

Example

The following *while* loop adds the numbers 1 through 10.

```
sum = 0;
i = 0;
while(i <= 10)
{
    sum += i;
    i++;
}
```

See Also

```
do, for, if, switch
```

2

The Microsoft C Compiler Features and Options

This chapter summarizes some of the features of Microsoft C related to the 8086 microprocessor, including the memory models and the Microsoft C compiler and linker options.

Memory Models in Microsoft C

A C compiler for the 8086 machines has two choices: Either it forces you to write programs that use only a single segment of data and code, or it can provide you with options to mix and match different addressing schemes for data and code. The concept of memory models arises from the availability of these choices. A specific memory model in Microsoft C refers to one of five ways of addressing code and data, shown in Table 2-1.

Table 2-1. Memory Models in the Microsoft C Compiler

Small	All data and code addresses are 16-bit offsets. Program size limited to one segment of code and one segment of data.
	Compiler option: /AS
	Note: This is the default in Microsoft C.
Medium	All data addresses are 16-bit offsets, but code addresses use explicit segment and offset. A program can have a single segment of data but many segments of code.
	Compiler option: /AM
Compact	All code addresses are offset only, but data addresses use segments as well as offsets. Programs can have multiple data segments but only one code segment.
	Compiler option: /AC
Large	All data and code addresses include explicit segment and offset. Program size is limited only by available memory

Table 2-1. (cont.)

	(which is limited by the 20-bit physical address), but a single data item cannot exceed a 64K segment.
	Compiler option: /AL
Huge	Same as the large model, but address arithmetic is performed in such a way that an array can span multiple segments.
	Compiler option: /AH

In addition to the five standard memory models, with keywords *far*, *near*, and *huge* you can mix data items with addressing scheme different from the default allowed by the standard model. These keywords can qualify the address of a data item as well as a function.

Predefined Global Variables

Microsoft C comes with a number of predefined global variables and preprocessor constants. The global variables contain the DOS version number, last error number, pointer to the process environment block, and other useful information. Table 2-2 summarizes the predefined global variables and their purpose.

Table 2-2. Predefined Global Variables in Microsoft C

Name	Declaration and Purpose
_amblksiz	*unsigned _amblksiz;*
	When the Microsoft C memory allocation routines have to allocate memory from the far heap, they first request memory from DOS in a big chunk and then they parcel out memory to satisfy calls made to *malloc* until the chunk is exhausted. The *_amblksiz* variable contains the size of a single chunk in bytes. The default value is 8192 bytes (or 8K). The *halloc* and the *_nmalloc* routines do not use this variable.
	Declared in: *malloc.h*
daylight	*int daylight;*
	The *daylight* variable is 1 if a daylight saving time zone is specified in the TZ environment variable. It is used when converting local time to Greenwich Mean Time. (See Chapter 12 for details.)
	Declared in: *time.h*
_doserrno	*int _doserrno;*
	Contains the MS-DOS error code returned by the last MS-DOS system call.
	Declared in: *stdlib.h*
environ	*char *environ[ ];*

Table 2-2. (cont.)

Name	Declaration and Purpose
	This is an array of pointers to strings where the strings constitute the environment table of the process. This allows you to access the environment variables for use by a particular program.
	Declared in: *stdlib.h*
errno	*int errno;*
	Contains an error code corresponding to the last system call.
	Declared in: *stdlib.h*
_fmode	*int _fmode;*
	Contains the default file translation mode. The default value is 0, which means files are translated in the text mode. (See *open* in Chapter 15 for more details.)
	Declared in: *stdlib.h*
_osmajor	*unsigned char _osmajor;*
	This is the major version number of MS-DOS. For example, if you have MS-DOS 3.30, *_osmajor* will be 3.
	Declared in: *stdlib.h*
_osminor	*unsigned char _osminor;* This is the minor version number of MS-DOS. For MS-DOS 3.10, *_osmajor* will be 10.
	Declared in: *stdlib.h*
_osversion	*unsigned _osversion;*
	This contains the complete DOS version number with the major version number in the lower byte and the minor version in the higher byte. For MS-DOS 3.20, *_osversion* will be 1403 in hexadecimal.
	Declared in: dos.h
_psp	*unsigned int _psp;*
	This variable contains the segment address of the program segment prefix (PSP) of the current process. The PSP contains information about the process such as the command-line arguments, pointer to the environment block, and the return address. The PSP begins at offset 0 of the segment address contained in *_psp*.
	Declared in: *stdlib.h*
sys_errlist	*char *sys_errlist[ ];*
	This is an array of pointers to a set of strings each corresponding to a system error message.
	Declared in: *stdlib.h*
sys_nerr	*int sys_nerr;*
	This is the total number of strings in the *sys_errlist* array.
	Declared in: *stdlib.h*
timezone	*long timezone;*

Table 2-2. (cont.)

Name	Declaration and Purpose
	The timezone variable contains the difference in seconds between Greenwich Mean Time and the local time. (See Chapter 12 for details.)
	Declared in: *time.h*
tzname	*char *tzname[2];*
	tzname[0] contains the name of the local time zone (for example, EST or PST) and tzname[1] contains the name of the daylight saving time zone. (See Chapter 12 for details.)
	Declared in: *time.h*

The Microsoft C 5.1 Compiler

Writing C code is only one aspect of developing software in Microsoft C. You have to compile the code, then link it with libraries to create the executable file, and, finally, debug the program when it fails to work properly. The Microsoft C 5.1 compiler comes with a set of tools that will help you in one or more of these steps. Both the compiler and the linker are accessed via a command-line-oriented program named CL.EXE, but the linker can also be invoked separately as LINK. Object modules are organized into libraries by the LIB utility. The MAKE utility lets you automate the steps involved in creating an executable file, helping you manage the *compile-link* cycle. Finally, the CodeView full-screen debugger helps you locate the *bugs* in your program.

CL—Compiling and Linking

CL is your gateway to both the compiler and the linker. For a small program with a few modules, you can compile the files and link them using CL as simply as

```
cl test.c rest.c
```

where we assume the main function to be in the file TEST.C and other functions in the file REST.C. Using the small memory model as the default, CL will create the object files TEST.OBJ and REST.OBJ and invoke the linker to generate the executable TEST.EXE.

Using CL without any options may be good enough for small test programs, but when you are developing a larger application, you will want to specify explicitly certain things such as the memory model, the type of math library you want to use, and whether you want the compiler to generate information needed by the CodeView debugger. You have to specify these choices through command-line options to CL. For example, we can use the following command to compile the example program using the large model, generate code for the 8087 math coprocessor, and also generate supporting information for the debugger:

```
CL /AL /FPi87 /Zi TEST.C REST.C
```

As you can see from the example, each option begins with a slash /. The next letter tells the compiler the type of the option, and subsequent characters and digits specify your complete choice for that type. In the example, the /AL option specifies the large memory model, the /FPi87 tells the compiler to embed 8087 code in the output, and the /Zi option generates the information needed to debug the executable with the CodeView debugger. Table 2-3 shows the options according to the purpose of each category. For example, all options relating to memory models are listed under the category named *memory model*. This should help you locate the options that relate to your specific need. The complete list of options for CL is quite extensive. (See Table 2-4.)

Table 2-3. Option Categories for CL

Purpose of Option	Options
Selecting a memory model DEFAULT: /AS	/AS /AM /AC /AL /AH
Selecting a floating-point library DEFAULT: /FPi	/FPa /FPc /FPC87 /FPi /FPi87
Controlling optimization DEFAULT: /Ot	/O /Oa /Od /Oi /Ol /On /Op /Or /Os /Ot /Ox
Controlling the preprocessor	/C /D⟨name⟩[=text] /E /EP /I⟨include path⟩ /P /u /U⟨name⟩ /X
Generating code for specific processor and mixed language calls DEFAULT: /G0	/G0 /G1 /G2 /Gc /Gm /Gs /Gt[number]
Specifying execution mode (real or OS/2 protected)	/Lp /Lr /Lc
CodeView support, error checking and language extensions DEFAULT: /Ze	/Za /Zd /Ze /Zg /Zi /Zl /Zs /Zp[1 or 2 or 4]
Creating listing, object, and executable files	/Fa[assembly file] /Fc[code file] /Fe⟨executable file ⟩ /Fl[listing file] /Fm[map file] /Fo⟨object file⟩ /Fs[source listing]
Formatting source listings	/Sl⟨column⟩ /Sp⟨lines⟩/Ss⟨subtitle⟩ /St⟨title⟩
Linking	/F⟨hex number⟩ /link ⟨linker options⟩
Miscellaneous	/c /H⟨number⟩ /J /Tc⟨file⟩ /ND⟨dataseg⟩ /NM⟨module⟩ /NT⟨textseg⟩ /V ⟨string⟩ /W⟨0 or 1 or 2 or 3⟩

Some of the options are straightforward, but a few, such as the optimization options (the /O family), are difficult to use. To use them intelligently, you need to understand the different types of optimizations that a compiler can perform and even have a general idea of how the compiler will react to your code. The best approach is to use the simple options in the beginning and then, as you learn more about the capabilities of the Microsoft C compiler, you can add the more exotic ones to your repertoire.

Table 2-4. List of Options for CL

Option	Action by CL
/AS	Selects small memory model (default).
/AM	Selects medium memory model.
/AC	Selects compact memory model.
/AL	Selects large memory model.
/AH	Selects huge memory model.
/A⟨string⟩	Sets up a customized memory model. The ⟨string⟩ consists of three characters, one from each group:

Group	Letter	Interpretation
Code size	s	Small
	l	Large
Data Size	n	Near
	f	Far
	h	Huge
Segments	d	SS is equal to DS
	u	SS not same as DS. DS loaded in each module.
	w	SS not same as DS. DS remains fixed.

Option	Action by CL
/C	Retains the comments when preprocessing file (valid with /E, /P, or /EP).
/c	Compiles without linking.
/D⟨name⟩[= text]	Defines the macro with the text. The equal sign and the following text may be omitted.
/E	Preprocesses a file and sends the output to *stdout* with line numbers.
/EP	Same as option /E, but no line numbers are printed.
/F⟨hex_ number⟩	Sets the stack size to number of bytes specified by the hexadecimal number.
/Fa[filename]	Sends an assembly listing to given file name. If file name is omitted, the default is the source file name with the extension .ASM.

Table 2-4. (cont.)

Option	Action by CL
/Fc[filename]	Generates a combined source-assembly listing.
/Fe⟨filename⟩	Accepts *filename* as the name of the executable file.
/Fl[filename]	Generates an object code listing.
/Fm[filename]	Generates a link map file.
/Fo⟨filename⟩	Accepts *filename* as the name of the object file.
/FPa	Generates calls to an alternate math library for floating-point operations.
/FPc	Generates calls to an emulator library for floating-point operations. At run-time, uses the 80x87 coproceccor, if one is found.
/FPc87	Generates calls to an 80x87 library. Requires 80x87 coprocessor at run-time.
/FPi	Generates in-line code that uses the emulator library. Uses 80x87 coprocessor at run-time, if one is found (default).
/FPi87	Generates in-line instructions for the 80x87 coprocessor. Requires an 80x87 at run-time.
/Fs[filename]	Produces a source listing.
/G0	Uses 8086 instructions (default).
/G1	Uses 80186 instructions.
/G2	Uses 80286 instructions.
/Gc	Uses Pascal-style function calls (arguments are pushed on stack in the order they appear in the function call and stack is cleaned up by the function before returning). This generates faster, compact code.
/Gm	Forces *near const* items to be allocated in the DATA segment. Used for generating ROM code. (Microsoft C 5.1 only.)
/Gs	Stack-checking calls are not generated.
/Gt[number]	Places data items larger than [number] bytes in a new data segment. Default [number] is 256.
/H⟨number⟩	Restricts significant characters in external names to specified length.
/HELP	Displays a list of commonly used CL options.
/I⟨pathname⟩	The ⟨pathname⟩ is added to the list of directories that are searched for include files.
/J	Changes the default type of char to unsigned.
/Lc	Compile for DOS 3.x compatibility mode (real mode). (Microsoft C 5.1 only.)
/Lp	Compile for OS/2 protected mode. (Microsoft C 5.1 only.)
/Lr	Synonym for /Lc. (Microsoft C 5.1 only.)
/link⟨options⟩	Passes the ⟨options⟩ to LINK.

Table 2-4. **(cont.)**

Option	Action by CL
/ND⟨dataseg⟩	Sets the name of the data segment to ⟨dataseg⟩.
/NM⟨module⟩	Sets the name of the module to ⟨module⟩.
/NT⟨textseg⟩	Sets the name of the code segment to ⟨textseg⟩.
/O	Enable optimization (same as /Ot).
/Oa	Ignores aliasing (multiple names for the same memory location).
/Od	Disables optimizations.
/Oi	Enables the use of intrinsic functions.
/Ol	Enables loop optimizations.
/On	Disables "unsafe" optimizations.
/Op	Enables precision optimizations on floating-point calculations.
/Or	Disables in-line return.
/Os	Optimizes for space.
/Ot	Optimizes for speed (default).
/Ox	Enables maximum optimization (same as /Oailt /Gs).
/P	Preprocesses and sends output to file with same name as source but with the extension .I.
/qc	Invokes the Microsoft QuickC compiler.
/Sl⟨columns⟩	Sets the characters per line in the source listings (should be between 79 and 132).
/Sp⟨lines⟩	Sets the page length in lines for source listings (should be between 15 and 255).
/Ss⟨string⟩	Sets the subtitle string for source listings.
/St⟨string⟩	Sets the title string for source listings.
/Tc⟨file⟩	Used to specify a ⟨file⟩ without the .c extension.
/U⟨name⟩	Removes predefined macro ⟨name⟩.
/u	Removes the definition of all predefined macros.
/V⟨string⟩	Puts a version string into the object file.
/W⟨number⟩	Sets the warning level for compiler warning messages. ⟨number⟩ is either 0 or 1 or 2 or 3.
/X	Ignores the list of "standard places" when searching for include files.
/Za	Enforces ANSI compatibilty by disabling all Microsoft extensions to the language.
/Zd	Generates line number information for the Microsoft SYMDEB symbolic debugger.
/Ze	Enables all features specific to Microsoft C (default).
/Zg	Generates function declarations without compiling program. The result is sent to the standard output.
/Zi	Generates symbolic debugging information

Table 2-4. (cont.)

Option	Action by CL
	required by Microsoft CodeView full-screen debugger.
/Zl	Removes default library information from the object files.
/Zp⟨n⟩	Packs structures on n-byte boundary.
/Zs	Performs a syntax check only.

Note: [. . .] denote optional items; ⟨ . . . ⟩ indicate required arguments.

It is tedious to type in the options you choose to use with CL to compile and link your program. Besides, you can enter only a maximum of 128 characters on the command line, which means that if you select a large number of options you will not be able to enter them on the command line to CL even if you were willing to key them. Microsoft C provides three ways to solve this problem.

You can define an environment variable CL (this is different from the executable CL) with the options you plan to use. For example, if we defined the CL environment variable by the DOS command:

```
SET CL=/AS /Gs /Od /Zi /FPc
```

then invoking the compiler with a *CL ⟨filename⟩* will be equivalent to the command *CL /AS /Gs /Od /Zi /FPc ⟨filename⟩*. Thus, the named program will be compiled and linked using the small model (/AS), without any stack-checking calls (/Gs), without any optimization (/Od), with support for CodeView (/Zi), and with calls to the floating-point emulator library.

Another approach is to place the compile command in a batch file that takes the file name as an argument and use the batch file to do the job. An example (using the same options as before) might be:

```
echo off
if not "%1" == "" goto run
:usage
echo ! usage:  RUN filename
echo !
echo ! where    filename is the program you are testing
echo !          (do not include extension, .C assumed)
echo !
goto end
:run
if exist %1.c goto filefound
echo ! RUN: File %1.c not found. Exiting...
goto end
:filefound
echo ! Now starting CL...
CL /AS /Gs /Od /Zi /FPc %1.c
:end
```

If this batch file is named RUN.BAT, you can compile and link a file TEST.C by the command *run test*. The batch file first checks if there is an argument present. If it finds the argument, it checks if the file named by the argument exists. If all goes well, RUN.BAT invokes CL using the options of your choice.

These two approaches are fine when you have the entire program in a single file. If you are working on a larger project, it is best to use the Microsoft MAKE utility. Microsoft MAKE is invoked by the command *MAKE ⟨makefile⟩* where ⟨*makefile*⟩ is the name of a file that contains the commands for MAKE. For a program that consists of several files, you will set up the MAKE commands to generate the object codes and then separately invoke LINK to build the executable. Apart from automating the building of an executable, MAKE also makes sure that it compiles only those modules that have changed since the last compilation. It does so by examining the time of last modification stamped on the files. A source file is compiled only if it was modified at a later time than the corresponding object file. We refer you to the documentation on MAKE included in the manuals distributed by Microsoft with their C compiler. Here is a short sample ⟨makefile⟩.

```
###############################################################
#    Makefile for Microsoft MAKE
#    Comments start with '#'
#
#    Model set to small
MODEL=S
# Compiler flags -- generate object code only (/c option)
CFLAGS=/A$(MODEL)      /Gs          /Od    /Zi  /FPc   /c
CL=cl $(CFLAGS)
# General inference rules
# Rule to make .OBJ files from .C files
.C.OBJ:
        $(CL) $*.C
# Compile the files
prog.obj: prog.c local.h common.h
file1.obj: file1.c common.h
file2.obj: file2.c local.h
# Make the executable
prog.exe:  prog.obj file1.obj file2.obj
        LINK $**, $@;
```

This MAKE file is for building a program named PROG.EXE, which has three source files: PROG.C, FILE1.C, and FILE2.C. There are two include files LOCAL.H and COMMON.H. The MAKE commands consist of dependency rules showing, for each file, the other files that it depends on. The dependency list is followed by a line showing how to prepare that file. If a generic rule is defined (for example, "build an .OBJ file out of a .C by using CL with the following options"), you do not have to state explicitly the command to build a file. In our sample make file, PROG.OBJ depends on the source files PROG.C, COM-

MON.H, and LOCAL.H, and PROG.EXE depends on the object files PROG.OBJ, FILE1.OBJ, and FILE2.OBJ. The LINK command to build the executable is explictly stated because we had not provided a rule to arrive at an executable from object modules.

LINK—The Linker

Although CL invokes the linker, you may sometimes want to invoke the linker alone, especially when no compilation is necessary. Also, in CL, the /link option allows you to specify linker options. So you need to know the command-line options for the linker as well. Table 2-5 describes the linker options together with their meaning.

Table 2-5. List of Options for LINK

Option	Action by LINK
/B[ATCH]	Disables prompting for path name when library or object file is not found.
/CO[DEVIEW]	Generates executable with information needed by Microsoft CodeView debugger.
/CP[ARMAXALLOC]:⟨num⟩	Sets the maximum number of 16-byte paragraphs needed by program to ⟨num⟩. Valid range for ⟨num⟩ is from 1 to 65,535.
/DO[SSEG]	Forces segments to be arranged in a particular order in memory. (Default when linking with a Microsoft library.)
/DS[ALLOCATE]	Forces loading of data at the high end of the data segment. Use this option with assembly language routines only.
/E[XEPACK]⟨exe⟩ ⟨pack⟩	Packs the executable ⟨exe⟩ during linking and places result in ⟨pack⟩
/F[ARCALLTRANSLATION]	Far calls within the same segment are converted to near calls. This makes calling far functions more efficient.
/HE[LP]	Lists the LINK options.
/HI[GH]	Places the executable file as high as possible in memory. Use this option with assembly language routines only.
/I[NFORMATION]	Displays informative messages during linking.
/LI[NENUMBERS]	Shows the line numbers of source statements in the map file.

Table 2-5. (cont.)

Option	Action by LINK
/M[AP]:[number]	Generates a listing of all global symbols in the input modules. The [number] denotes the maximum number of symbols the linker can sort.
/NOD[EFAULTLIBRARYSEARCH]	Ignores default libraries.
/NOE[XTDICTIONARY]	Accepts a user-defined substitute for a standard library function.
/NOF[ARCALLTRANSLATION]	Turns off the /FARCALLTRANSLATION option (default).
/NOG[ROUPASSOCIATION]	Provided only for compatibility with early versions of linker and compiler.
/NOI[GNORECASE]	Begins distinguishing between uppercase and lowercase letters.
/NOP[ACKCODE]	Turns off the /PACKCODE option (default).
/O[VERLAYINTERRUPT]:⟨num⟩	Sets up ⟨num⟩ as the interrupt number to be used when an overlay has to be loaded.
/PAC[KCODE]	Packs adjacent code segments into 64K chunks (use with /FARCALLTRANSLATION).
/PAU[SE]	Pauses before writing executable to disk, thus allowing you to swap diskettes.
/Q[UICKLIBRARY]	Produces a library for use with Microsoft QuickC compiler.
/SE[GMENTS]:⟨number⟩	Sets the maximum number of segments to ⟨number⟩, default is 128.
/ST[ACK]:⟨number⟩	Sets the stack size to ⟨number⟩ bytes, default is 2048 bytes (2K).

Note: [. . .] denote optional items, ⟨ . . . ⟩ indicate required arguments

II
Microsoft C Process Control and Memory Management

3

Process Control

The process control routines include the signal-handling routines that take care of error conditions and the utility routines that terminate a process, communicate with the operating system, and execute stand-alone programs as child processes. The routines described in this chapter are defined in *signal.h*, *setjmp.h*, and *stdlib.h*.

A process is an executable program in memory and its associated environment. Any time you run a program, you create a process. The environment of a process includes all the information necessary to execute the process. The exact interpretation of the environment differs from one system to another. In UNIX and MS-DOS, it includes a list of strings that contains definitions of environment variables.

Signals are the operating system's way of interrupting a process when certain error conditions or "exceptions" occur. The signal mechanism is present in UNIX and is supported by most C libraries, including the Microsoft C library. You can use the library routine *signal* to install a routine to handle a particular signal. When that exception occurs, the handler for that signal will be called. The *raise* function can be used to generate a signal explicitly.

► abort

Purpose

Use *abort* to print an error message to *stderr* and abnormally exit your program by calling *_exit(3)*.

Syntax

```
#include <stdlib.h>
void abort(void);
```

Example Call

```
abort();
```

See Also

```
atexit, exit, _exit, onexit, raise, signal
```

► assert

Purpose

Use the *assert* macro to print an error message and abort the program if the ⟨expression⟩ is false. You can disable *assert* by defining the preprocessor macro NDEBUG before including the file *assert.h*.

Syntax

```
#include <assert.h>
void assert(<expression>);
<expression>       C statements specifying assertion being tested
```

Example Call

```
assert(arg_value >= 0);
```

See Also

```
abort
```

► atexit, onexit

Purpose

Use *atexit* or *onexit* to set up a stack of up to 32 functions that

atexit, onexit

will be called in a LIFO manner when your program terminates normally. This feature is useful for setting up "house-cleaning" chores that should be performed when your application exits.

Syntax

```
#include <stdlib.h>
int atexit(void (*func2)(void));
onexit_t onexit(onexit_t func2);
void (*func1)(void);    Pointer to function to be called
onexit_t func2;         onexit_t is defined to be a pointer to a function
                        returning an integer
```

Example Call

```
atexit(cleanup_all);
onexit(close_files);
```

Returns

The *atexit* function returns a zero if successful. Otherwise, it returns a nonzero value. The *onexit* function returns its argument, if successful. It returns NULL in case of any error.

See Also

```
exit
```

Example

Line 18 in Example 3-1 installs the function *cleanup* that will be called when the program exits by calling *exit*.

cwait, wait ◄

Purpose

Use the *cwait* and *wait* functions in OS/2's protected mode to wait for a child process. The *cwait* function waits until a specified child process terminates, while *wait* waits until any one of your immediate child processes terminate. These functions are available in Microsoft C 5.1 only.

Syntax

```
#include <process.h>
int cwait(int *p_status, int proc_id, int action);
int wait(int *p_status);
int *p_status;    Address of integer to hold termination status code
int proc_id;      Process identification number of child
int action;       Action code to indicate whether cwait waits for child
                  alone (WAIT_CHILD) or for all grandchildren too
                  (WAIT_GRANDCHILD)
```

Example Call

```
pid = spawnv(P_NOWAIT, "child.exe", args);
if (cwait(&status, pid, WAIT_GRANDCHILD) == -1)
                perror("cwait failed");
if (wait(&status) == -1) perror("wait failed");
```

Returns

Upon normal termination both functions return the process identification of the child. In case of error or abnormal termination, they return −1 and set *errno* to an appropriate error code.

See Also

```
spawn functions
```

► execl, execle, execlp, execlpe, execv, execve, execvp, execvpe

---

Purpose

Use any one of the exec functions to load and execute a child process in the memory currently occupied by your program's code. The name of the executable file is given in the argument *path*. The other arguments depend on the version of exec function used.

Syntax

```
#include <process.h>
int execl(char *path, char *arg0, char *arg1,..., NULL);
int execle(char *path, char *arg0, char *arg1,..., NULL,
          char *envp[]);
int execlp(char *path, char *arg0, char *arg1,..., NULL);
int execlpe(char *path, char *arg0, char *arg1,..., NULL,
            char *envp[]);
int execv(char *path, char *argv[]);
int execve(char *path, char *argv[], char *envp[]);
int execvp(char *path, char *argv[]);
int execvpe(char *path, char *argv[], char *envp[]);
```

`char *path;`	*Path name of file to be executed as a child process*
`char *arg0, *arg1, ..., NULL;`	*Command-line arguments for the child process (ends with a NULL)*
`char *argv[];`	*Array of command-line arguments for the child process*
`char *envp[];`	*Environment table for child process*

Example Call

```
execv("child.exe", argv);
```

execl, ..., execvpe

Returns

If successful, the exec functions do not return to their parent. If an error occurs, the return value is −1, and the global variable *errno* is set to an error code.

See Also

spawn functions

exit, __exit ◀

Purpose

Use *exit* to terminate your program normally by flushing file buffers, closing files, and invoking functions set up with *atexit* or *onexit*. The __exit function also terminates a process, but it does not flush buffers or call routines set up by *atexit* or *onexit*.

Syntax

```
#include <stdlib.h>
void exit(int status);
void _exit(int status);
int  status;        Exit status code
```

Example Call

```
exit(0);
```

See Also

abort, atexit, onexit

Example

Lines 23, 51, 60, and 71 in Example 3-1 show calls to *exit*.

getenv ◀

Purpose

Use *getenv* to get the definition of the environment variable *varname* from the environment of the process.

Syntax

```
#include <stdlib.h>
char *getenv(const char *varname);
const char *varname;        Name of environment variable to look for
```

Example Call

```
current_path = getenv("PATH");
```

Returns

If *varname* is found, *getenv* returns a pointer to the string value of *varname*. If *varname* is undefined, *getenv* will return a NULL.

See Also

putenv

▶ getpid

Purpose

Use *getpid* to obtain the "process ID," an integer value that identifies the calling process.

Syntax

```
#include <process.h>
int getpid(void);
```

Example Call

```
pid = getpid();
```

See Also

cwait, wait

▶ longjmp

Purpose

Use the *longjmp* function to restore the calling environment to that contained in the *jmp_buf* array *env*. This environment must have been saved by an earlier call to *setjmp*. The *longjmp* function restores all local variables (except the ones declared *volatile*) to their previous states and returns as if from the last call to *setjmp* with the return value *retval*.

Since *longjmp* jumps to the return address of the last matching call to *setjmp*, you must make sure that the call to *longjmp* occurs before the function where you called *setjmp* has returned.

Syntax

```
#include <setjmp.h>
void longjmp(jmp_buf env, int retval);
jmp_buf env;        Array data type where the calling environment is stored
```

longjmp

| int | retval; | *Value that will appear to be returned by the earlier call to* setjmp |

Example Call

```
longjmp(stack_env, 1);
```

See Also

setjmp

Example

Line 75 in Example 3-1 calls *longjmp* to return to the main command loop when the user presses Ctrl-C.

perror ◀

Purpose

Use *perror* to construct an error message by concatenating your message provided in the argument *string* with that from the system corresponding to the current value in the global variable *errno*, and print the message to *stderr*.

Syntax

```
#include <stdio.h>
void perror(const char *string);
const char *string;      Your part of the message
```

Example Call

```
perror("Error closing file");
```

See Also

_strerror, strerror

Example

Line 22 in Example 3-1 uses *perror* to display an error message.

putenv ◀

Purpose

Use *putenv* to add the definition *newdef* to the environment of the process.

Syntax

```
#include <stdlib.h>
int putenv(const char *newdef);
const char *newdef;          Definition to be added to environment table
```

Example Call

```
putenv("PATH=C:\\BIN");
```

Returns

If successful, *putenv* returns a 0; otherwise, it returns −1.

See Also

```
getenv
```

 raise

Purpose

Use *raise* to "raise a signal" that creates an exception condition corresponding to the number *signum*.

Syntax

```
#include <signal.h>
int raise(int signum);
int signum;      Signal number to be raised
```

Example Call

```
raise(SIGABRT);
```

Returns

If successful, *raise* returns a zero. Otherwise, it returns a non-zero value.

See Also

```
abort, signal
```

 setjmp

Purpose

Use the *setjmp* function to save a stack environment in the *jmp _buf* array named *env* before calling another function. This environment can subsequently be restored by a call to

setjmp

longjmp, achieving the effect of a nonlocal *goto*. When *longjmp* is called at a later time with the saved calling environment, it restores all stack based local variables in the routine to the values they had when *setjmp* was called and jumps to the return address that *setjmp* had saved. Note that this process does not guarantee the proper restoration of register-based and *volatile* variables.

Syntax

```
#include <setjmp.h>
int setjmp(jmp_buf env);
jmp_buf env;       Array data type where the current calling environment is
                   stored
```

Example Call

```
if (setjmp(env) != 0) printf("Returned from longjmp\n");
```

Returns

After saving the stack environment *setjmp* returns 0. When *longjmp* is called with the environment saved by this particular call to *setjmp*, the effect is the same as returning from *setjmp* again, this time with the second argument of *longjmp* as the return value.

See Also

```
longjmp
```

Example

Line 30 in Example 3-1 establishes a mark in the main program to which we can jump from any place in the program by calling *longjmp*.

---

signal ◀

Purpose

Use the *signal* function to set up the routine *func* as the handler for the exception or signal number *signum*. The handler is expected to accept the signal number as an argument. The signal number *signum* must be one of the constants shown in Table 3-1. These constants are defined in the include file *signal.h*. If you want to ignore a signal, use SIG_IGN as the second argument to *signal*. Specifying SIG_DFL as the second argument sets up the implementation-defined default handling for the signal. Under OS/2, SIG_ACK may be used as the second argument to *signal* to signify that OS/2 must not send a signal until a SIG_ACK acknowledgment is received for the last signal.

Table 3-1. List of Signals in Microsoft C 5.1

Signal	Exception Condition
SIGABRT	Abnormal termination of program, for example, by calling the *abort* function.
SIGBREAK	Ctrl-Break signal. Default action is to terminate process. (Microsoft C 5.1 only.)
SIGFPE	Floating-point error, such as overflow and division by zero.
SIGILL	Illegal instruction in the program.
SIGINT	Generated when user presses a key designed to get the attention of the operating system. For example, pressing Ctrl-C in UNIX or MS-DOS would generate this signal.
SIGSEGV	Illegal memory access.
SIGUSR1	OS/2 Process flag A. (Microsoft C 5.1 only.)
SIGUSR2	OS/2 Process flag B. (Microsoft C 5.1 only.)
SIGUSR3	OS/2 Process flag C. (Microsoft C 5.1 only.)
SIGTERM	Termination request sent to the program.

Syntax

```
#include <signal.h>
void (*signal(int signum, void (*func)(int)))(int);
int signum;          Signal number for which a handler is being set up
void (*func)(int);   Pointer to handler that can accept an integer
                     argument or one of the constants SIG_DFL, SIG_
                     IGN, or SIG_ACK
```

Example Call

```
if(signal(SIGINT, ctrlc_handler) == SIG_ERR)
{
    perror("signal failed");
    exit(0);
}
```

Returns

If successful, *signal* returns the pointer to the previous handler. In case of error, it returns the constant SIG_ERR and sets the global variable *errno* to to an error constant.

See Also

```
abort, raise
```

Example

Lines 20, 68, and 73 in Example 3-1 illustrate the use of *signal* to handle the SIGINT signal.

signal

spawnl, spawnle, spawnlp, spawnlpe, ◀ spawnv, spawnve, spawnvp, spawnvpe

Purpose

Use any one of the spawn functions to load and execute a child process and return to your program when the child process terminates. The name of the executable file is given in the argument *path*. The mode of execution of the child process is specified by the *modeflag* argument. Under MS-DOS, this flag can take one of two values: P_WAIT or P_OVERLAY. The P_WAIT flag indicates that the parent process should be suspended until the child completes, whereas P_OVERLAY means that the child overwrites the parent in memory destroying the parent. The P_OVERLAY mode has the same effect as calling the exec functions. Under OS/2, you can use P_NOWAIT as *modeflag* to signify that the execution of the child process should proceed concurrently with the parent. The rest of the arguments depend on the version of spawn function used.

Syntax

```
#include <process.h>
int spawnl(int modeflag, char *path, char *arg0, char *arg1,
          ..., NULL);
int spawnle(int modeflag, char *path, char *arg0, char *arg1,
          ..., NULL, char *envp[]);
int spawnlp(int modeflag, char *path, char *arg0, char *arg1,
          ..., NULL);
int spawnlpe(int modeflag, char *path, char *arg0, char
          *arg1,..., NULL, char *envp[]);
int spawnv(int modeflag, char *path, char *argv[]);
int spawnve(int modeflag, char *path, char *argv[], char
          *envp[]);
int spawnvp(int modeflag, char *path, char *argv[]);
int spawnvpe(int modeflag, char *path, char *argv[], char
          *envp[]);
```

int modeflag;	*Execution mode of calling process*
char *path;	*Path name of file to be executed as a child process*
char *arg0, *arg1, ..., NULL;	*Command-line arguments for the child process (ends with a NULL)*
char *argv[];	*Array of command-line arguments for the child process*
char *envp[];	*Environment table for child process*

Example Call

```
spawnvpe(P_WAIT, "child.exe", argv, envp);
```

Returns

If an error occurs, the return value is −1 and the global variable *errno* is set to an error code. When P_WAIT is used as the *modeflag*, the spawn functions return the exit status of the child process to the parent. The return value for P_NOWAIT is the process ID of the child process.

See Also

exec functions

▶ system

Purpose

Use *system* to execute an MS-DOS command contained in *string* from your program.

Syntax

```
#include <stdlib.h>
int system(const char *string);
const char *string;        Command to be executed
```

Example Call

```
system("DIR");
```

Returns

If *string* is not NULL, *system* returns zero if the command was successfully executed. In case of error, it returns −1 and sets *errno* to an error code. If *string* is NULL, *system* returns a non-zero value only if COMMAND.COM is present in the environment.

Example 3-1   The pair *setjmp* and *longjmp* is ideal for error handling or handling special conditions in a program. You call *setjmp* at a place where you have code that you may want to execute later. Then, whenever your conditions are met, call *longjmp* with the *jmp_buf* variable saved earlier by *setjmp*. This places you where *setjmp* was called originally. It appears as though the *setjmp* function returned a second time, this time with the value from the second argument to *longjmp*. Here is a small program to illustrate a way to use this versatile duo. Notice how *atexit* is used to set up a function that handles house-cleaning chores before exiting the program. The program also establishes signal handling for the Ctrl-C keypress (SIGINT signal).

system

```
 1:#include <stdio.h>
 2:#include <signal.h>
 3:#include <setjmp.h>
 4:
 5:static int ctrlc_handler(int);
 6:static void cleanup(void);
 7:
 8:/* Buffer used by setjmp and longjmp */
 9:jmp_buf main_menu;
10:
11:static FILE *datafile = NULL;
12:
13:main()
14:{
15:    char input[80];
16:    int choice=0;
17:/* Install routine to be called by 'exit' */
18:    atexit(cleanup);
19:/* Take over the Ctrl-C interrupt */
20:    if(signal(SIGINT, ctrlc_handler) == SIG_ERR)
21:    {
22:     perror("signal failed");
23:     exit(1);
24:    }
25:    printf("Installed SIGINT signal handler\n");
26:
27:/* Call 'setjmp' to set up for returning to this
28: * point after user presses Ctrl-C
29: */
30:    if(setjmp(main_menu) != 0)
31:    {
32:/* Returning from a 'longjmp' -- print message */
33:        printf("Interrupted...\n");
34:        fflush(stdin);  /*  flush input buffer */
35:    }
36:
37:/* This is the main menu of the program */
38:    printf("1  Loop endlessly...\n"
39:            "anything else to exit\n\n"
40:            "Enter Choice: ");
41:    gets(input);
42:    choice = atoi(input);
43:    switch(choice)
44:    {
45:        case 1:
46:            printf("Enter name of file to open: ");
47:            gets(input);
48:            if ((datafile = fopen(input,"r")) == NULL)
49:            {
50:                printf("Error opening %s\n", input);
51:                exit(2);
52:            }
```

```
53:
54:/* The next line is an endless loop - simulates a
55: * process gone awry.
56: */
57:          for(;;) printf("Looping..."
58:                         "press ^C to interrupt\n");
59:
60:       default: exit(0);
61:    }
62:}
63:/*----------------------------------------------------*/
64:int ctrlc_handler(int sig)
65:{
66:    int c;
67:/* First arrange to ignore further SIGINT */
68:    signal(SIGINT, SIG_IGN);
69:    printf("\nInterrupted. Quit?");
70:    c = getchar();
71:    if(c == 'y' || c == 'Y') exit(0);
72:/* Reenable interrupt handler -- and return */
73:    signal(SIGINT, ctrlc_handler);
74:/* Return to the main menu--to place marked by setjmp*/
75:    longjmp(main_menu, 1);
76:}
77:/*----------------------------------------------------*/
78:void cleanup(void)
79:{
80:/* This routine handles the "house-cleaning" chores */
81:    puts("Cleaning up...");
82:    if (datafile != NULL) fclose(datafile);
83:}
```

4

Variable Arguments

In writing C programs, you encounter functions such as *printf* that can take a variable number of arguments. Sometimes it is convenient to be able to write your own routines that can process a variable number of arguments. Take, for instance, a routine (*findmax*) that picks the largest from an array of integers. If the routine can accept a variable number of arguments, you can use such calls as *findmax(1,2,3)* and *findmax(a,b,c,d)* to find the maximum of any number of arguments. A set of macros in Microsoft C makes a straightforward task of handling a variable number of arguments. There are two sets of macros: One set conforming to the proposed ANSI standard is defined in the header file *stdarg.h*, and the other UNIX System V compatible set is defined in *varargs.h*.

► va__arg, va__end, va__start   *ANSI version*

Purpose

Use the *va__start*, *va__arg*, and *va__end* macros to access the arguments of a function when it takes a fixed number of required arguments followed by a variable number of optional arguments. The required arguments are in standard style and accessed by parameter name. The optional arguments are accessed using the macros *va__start*, *va__arg*, and *va__end*. See Example 4-1 for a typical use of these macros.

Syntax

```
#include <stdarg.h>
<type> va_arg(va_list arg_ptr, <type>);
void va_end(va_list arg_ptr);
void va_start(va_list arg_ptr, prev_param);
va_list arg_ptr;      Pointer to list of arguments
prev_param            Name of parameter just preceding first optional
                      argument
<type>                Type of argument to be retrieved, for example char *
```

Example Call

```
va_start(argp, firstint);
first_x = firstint;
next_x = va_arg(argp, int);
```

Returns

The *va__arg* macro returns a pointer to the next argument of given type. The *va__start* macro sets a pointer to the beginning of the list of arguments.

See Also

```
vfprintf, vprintf, vsprintf
```

Example

Example 4-1 demonstrates the ANSI-style macros for handling variable-length argument lists.

► va__arg, va__end, va__start   *UNIX V version*

Purpose

The *va__start*, *va__arg*, and *va__end* macros defined in

va__arg, va__end, va__start

varargs.h are similar to the ANSI version of the macros. They differ in the way the function using the macros is declared.

Syntax

```
#include <varargs.h>
<type> va_arg(arg_ptr, <type>);
void va_end(va_list arg_ptr);
void va_start(va_list arg_ptr);
va_alist              Macro that must appear at the end of all required
                      arguments to the function
va_dcl                Declaration of va__alist
va_list arg_ptr;      Pointer to list of arguments
<type>                Type of argument to be retrieved, for example char *
```

Example Call

```
char *findlongest(va_alist)
va_dcl                 /* Must appear without semicolon*/
{
    char *next_str;    /* Assume arguments are strings */
    va_alist argp;
    va_start(argp);
    while((next_str = va_arg(argp, char*)) != NULL)
        printf("Next string is: %s\n", next_str);
}
```

Returns

The *va_arg* macro returns a pointer to the next argument of given type. The *va_start* macro sets a pointer to the beginning of the list of arguments.

See Also

vfprintf, vprintf, vsprintf

Example 4-1   Demonstrate the use of variable length argument processing by writing a function that accepts a variable number of integer arguments and returns the largest value. Assume that a value of −999 marks the end of the argument list. Write a main program that shows how the function is used.

```
#include <stdio.h>
#include <stdarg.h>
int findmax(int, ...);
main()
{
    int maxvalue;
/* The end of the list of integers is marked by -9999 */
    maxvalue = findmax(-1, 20, 30, 50, -9999);
    printf("findmax(-1, 20, 30, 50, -9999) returns: \
    %d\n", maxvalue);
```

va__arg, va__end, va__start

```
    maxvalue = findmax(1, 2, 3, 4, 5, 6, 7, 8, -9999);
    printf("findmax(1, 2, 3, 4, 5, 6, 7, 8, -9999)\
returns: %d\n", maxvalue);
}
/*------------------------------------------------------*/
/* The "findmax" finds the largest value in a list
 * of integers. It uses the "va_..." macros to get
 * the arguments. This is the ANSI version.
 */
int findmax(int firstint, ...)
{
    int maxval = -9999, x = 0;
    va_list argp;
/* Get the first optional parameter using "va_start" */
    va_start(argp, firstint);
    x = firstint;
    while(x != -9999)
    {
            if(maxval < x) maxval = x;
          x = va_arg(argp, int);
    }
    return (maxval);
}
```

5
Memory Allocation

The memory allocation functions give you all the memory management tools necessary for building complex applications that use the available memory intelligently. You need memory allocation capabilities when you cannot determine in advance the exact amount of space you will need to store the data used or generated in your program. Although ANSI C supports only four basic memory management routines—*calloc*, *free*, *malloc*, and *realloc*—Microsoft C has an additional 25 routines that are necessary because of the variety of memory models supported by Microsoft C. The prototypes for these routines appear in *malloc.h*.

► alloca

Purpose

Use *alloca* to obtain *n* bytes of space in the program's stack for temporary use.

Syntax

```
#include <malloc.h>
void *alloca(size_t n);
size_t n;      Number of bytes to be allocated from the stack
```

Example Call

```
ptr = alloca(80); /* Allocate 80 bytes on the stack */
```

Returns

The *alloca* function returns a pointer to the first byte of the space allocated on the stack. If the function fails because of insufficient space on the stack, a NULL is returned.

See Also

```
calloc, malloc, stackavail
```

► calloc

Purpose

Use *calloc* to allocate memory for an array of *num_elems* elements each of size *elem_size* bytes and initialize them to 0.

Syntax

```
#include <stdlib.h>    or    #include <malloc.h>
void *calloc(size_t num_elems, size_t elem_size);
size_t   num_elems;         Number of elements
size_t   elem_size;         Size of each element in bytes
```

Example Call

```
p_int = (int *) calloc(100, sizeof(int));
```

Returns

The *calloc* function returns a pointer to the allocated memory. In case of error, a NULL is returned.

See Also

```
free, malloc, realloc
```

Example

Line 9 in Example 5-1 uses *calloc* to allocate a buffer.

__expand ◄

Purpose

Use *_expand* to enlarge or shrink a previously allocated block of memory, without moving the location of the block in the heap.

Syntax

```
#include <malloc.h>
void *_expand(void *mem_address, size_t newsize);
void *mem_address;      Pointer to previously allocated block of memory
size_t newsize;         Requested size of block in number of bytes
```

Example Call

```
_expand(p_old_block, 2000*sizeof(int));
```

Returns

When successful, *_expand* returns the argument *mem_address*. Otherwise, it returns NULL.

See Also

```
realloc
```

__ffree, free, __nfree ◄

Purpose

Use the *free* function to deallocate (return to the pool of free memory) a block of memory that was allocated earlier by *malloc*, *calloc*, or *realloc*. The *_ffree* and *_nfree* functions are versions of *free* meant for deallocating blocks in the far and the near heaps, respectively. The *_ffree* and *_nfree* functions are meant for use in mixed-model programming. For example, in a small model you can use *_ffree* to free a data item allocated on the far heap by *_fmalloc*.

Syntax

```
#include <malloc.h>
```

```
void _ffree(void far  *far_ptr);
void free(void *mem_address);
void _nfree(void near  *near_ptr);
void *mem_address;        Pointer to block of memory to be released
void far *far_ptr;        Far pointer to block to be freed by _ffree
void near *near_ptr;      Near pointer to block to be freed by _nfree
```

Example Call

```
free(buffer);
_ffree(far_buffer);
_nfree(near_buffer);
```

See Also

```
calloc, _fmalloc, malloc, _nmalloc, realloc
```

Example

Lines 38 and 39 in Example 5-1 use *free* to deallocate memory.

► __fheapchk, heapchk, __nheapchk

Purpose

Use _*heapchk* to check the consistency of the heap, the linked list of memory blocks from which functions such as *malloc* allocate memory. This is meant to be a debugging tool to pinpoint problems related to memory allocation from the heap. The Microsoft C compiler maps _*heapchk* to _*fheapchk* in large and compact memory models and to _*nheapchk* in small and medium models.

Syntax

```
#include <malloc.h>
int _fheapchk(void);   /* For far heap    */
int _heapchk(void);    /* Generic version */
int _nheapchk(void);   /* For near heap   */
```

Example Call

```
if(_heapchk() != _HEAPOK)
        printf("Heap consistency check failed!\n");
```

Returns

These routines return an integer indicating the results of the consistency check. Table 5-1 shows the possible values.

See Also

```
_fheapset, _fheapwalk, _heapset, _heapwalk, _nheapset,
_nheapwalk
```

Table 5-1. Results of Heap Consistency Check

Constant	Interpretation
_HEAPOK	All heap entries appear to be correct.
_HEAPEMPTY	Heap has not been initialized.
_HEAPBADBEGIN	The initial header information could not be found.
_HEAPBADNODE	A node in the heap's linked list is bad.

_fheapset, _heapset, _nheapset ◄

Purpose

Use _heapset to fill each byte in unused portion of the heap with the character given in *fill_char*. This is meant to be a debugging tool to pinpoint problems related to memory allocation from the heap. The Microsoft C compiler maps _heapset to _fheapset in large and compact memory models and to _nheapset in small and medium models.

Syntax

```
#include <malloc.h>
int _fheapset(unsigned fill_char);    /* For far heap    */
int _heapset(unsigned fill_char);     /* Generic version */
int _nheapset(unsigned fill_char);    /* For near heap   */
unsigned fill_char;        Character used to fill unused memory in the heap
```

Example Call

```
if(_heapset('N') != _HEAPOK)
        printf("Heap consistency check failed!\n");
```

Returns

These functions return same values as _heapchk. (See Table 5-1.)

See Also

```
_fheapchk, _fheapwalk, _heapchk, _heapwalk, _nheapchk,
_nheapwalk
```

_fheapwalk, _heapwalk, _nheapwalk ◄

Purpose

Use _heapwalk to traverse the entries in the heap, the pool of free memory blocks from which functions such as *malloc* allocate memory. Each call to _*heapwalk* returns information about the address of the next block of memory in the heap, its size, and whether it is free or in use. The information is returned in a _*heapinfo* structure, which is defined in *malloc.h* as:

```
struct _heapinfo
{
    int far *_pentry;   /* Pointer to next entry          */
    size_t  _size;      /* Size of this block in bytes    */
    int     _useflag;   /* Flag: _USEDENTRY or _FREEENTRY */
};
```

Syntax

```
#include <malloc.h>
int _fheapwalk(struct _heapinfo *heap_entry);   /* For far
                                                      heap    */
int _heapwalk(struct _heapinfo *heap_entry);    /* Generic
                                                   version */
int _nheapwalk(struct _heapinfo *heap_entry);   /* For near
                                                      heap    */
struct _heapinfo *heap_entry;      Pointer to structure that holds
                                   information about heap entry
```

Example Call

```
if(_heapwalk(&heapentry) == _HEAPOK)
    printf("Address: %p Status; %6s Size: %5u\n",
        heapentry._pentry, (heapentry._useflag == _FREEENTRY ?
        "FREE" : "UNUSED"), heapentry._size);
```

Returns

The heap traversal functions return the same values as _*heapchk*. (See Table 5-1.) Additionally, a return value of _HEAPBADPTR indicates a bad value in the _*pentry* field and that of _HEAPEND means that the end of the heap was reached.

See Also

_fheapchk, _fheapset, _heapchk, _heapset, _nheapchk, _nheapset

---

► _fmalloc, malloc, _nmalloc

Purpose

Use the *malloc* function to allocate the number of bytes requested in the argument *num_bytes*. Use _*fmalloc* and _*nmalloc* when you explicitly want to allocate memory from the far and near heap, respectively. The Microsoft C compiler automatically uses _*fmalloc* in the large and compact memory models and _*nmalloc* in the small and medium models. You can use *_fmalloc* and *_nmalloc* when you have far and near data items. For example, you can use *_fmalloc* to allocate from the far heap in a small memory program.

Syntax

```
#include <malloc.h>
void far *_fmalloc(size_t num_bytes);
void *malloc(size_t num_bytes);
void near *_nmalloc(size_t num_bytes);
size_t   num_bytes;     Number of bytes needed
```

Example Call

```
buffer = (char *)malloc(100*sizeof(char));
far_buf = (double *)_fmalloc(2048*sizeof(double));
near_buf = (short *)_nmalloc(16*sizeof(short));
```

Returns

If successful, each function returns a pointer, which is the starting address of the allocated memory. Otherwise, it returns a NULL.

See Also

```
_ffree, free, calloc, _nfree, realloc
```

Example

Line 20 in Example 5-1 uses *malloc* to allocate room for a buffer.

__fmsize, __msize, __nmsize ◀

Purpose

Use the *_msize* function to determine the size, in number of bytes, of a block of memory that has been allocated or manipulated by *malloc*, *calloc*, or *realloc*. In small and medium memory models, *_msize* is mapped to *_nmsize*, and in the compact and large models it maps to *_fmsize*.

Syntax

```
#include <malloc.h>
size_t _fmsize(void far *far_address);
size_t _msize(void *mem_address);
size_t _nmsize(void near *near_address);
void far *far_address;      Pointer to previously allocated block of
                            memory in the far heap
void *mem_address;          Pointer to previously allocated block of
                            memory whose size is to be determined
```

```
void near *near_address;        Pointer to previously allocated block of
                                memory in the near heap
```

Example Call

```
blocksize = _msize(p_block);
```

Returns

Each function returns the number of bytes allocated in the specified block of memory.

See Also

```
_memavl, _memmax
```

 **__freect**

Purpose

Use the *__freect* function to determine the approximate number
of elements of a given size that can be allocated in the default
data segment.

Syntax

```
#include <malloc.h>
unsigned int _freect(size_t elem_size);
size_t elem_size;       Size of each data element in bytes
```

Example Call

```
room_for_integers = _freect(sizeof(int));
```

Returns

The *__freect* returns the number of items of *elem __size* bytes that
can be allocated in the default data segment.

See Also

```
_memavl, _memmax
```

---

 halloc

Purpose

Use *halloc* to allocate memory for an array of data elements
when the total size of requested memory exceeds the size of a
64K segment. The allocation is done by calling the MS-DOS

halloc

memory allocation function (function number 48H). You should use *hfree* to free the memory allocated by *halloc*.

Syntax

```
#include <malloc.h>
void huge *halloc(long num_elems, size_t elem_size);
long      num_elems;    Number of elements
size_t    elem_size;    Size of each element in bytes
```

Example Call

```
p_huge = (short huge *)halloc(100000, sizeof(short));
```

Returns

If successful, the *halloc* function returns a *huge* pointer to the first byte of the allocated array. Otherwise, it returns NULL.

See Also

```
_dos_allocmem, _dos_freemem, hfree
```

hfree ◄

Purpose

Use the *hfree* function to release a block of memory previously allocated by *halloc*. The memory is released by calling the MS-DOS memory deallocation function 49H.

Syntax

```
#include <malloc.h>
void hfree(void huge *mem_address);
void huge *mem_address;    Pointer to block of memory to be released
```

Example Call

```
hfree((void huge *)bigbuf);
```

See Also

```
_dos_allocmem, _dos_freemem, halloc
```

__memavl, __memmax ◄

Purpose

Use the *__memavl* function to determine the number of bytes available in the default data segment beyond the space already being used by the program's data. The *_memmax* function, on the other hand, tells you the maximum number of contiguous bytes that can be allocated from the default data segment.

Syntax

```
#include <malloc.h>
size_t _memavl(void);
size_t _memmax(void);
```

Example Call

```
available_memory = _memavl();
max_single_block_size = _memmax();
```

Returns

The *_memavl* function returns the total number of bytes available for allocation in the default data segment, while *_memmax* returns the size of the largest contiguous block.

See Also

```
_fmsize, _freect, _msize, _nmsize
```

▶ realloc

Purpose

Use the *realloc* function to alter the size of a previously allocated block of memory at *mem_address* to the new size given in the argument *newsize*.

Syntax

```
#include <stdlib.h>    or    #include <malloc.h>
void *realloc(void *mem_address, size_t newsize);
void *mem_address;     Pointer to the block of memory whose size is to be
                       altered
size_t   newsize;      New size of the block in bytes
```

Example Call

```
new_buffer = realloc(old_buffer, old_size+100);
```

Returns

The *realloc* function returns the address of the block of memory. If *realloc* fails, it returns a NULL.

See Also

```
calloc, free, malloc
```

realloc

Example

Line 30 in Example 5-1 uses *realloc* to enlarge the size of an allocated buffer.

---

sbrk ◀

Purpose

Use *sbrk* to alter the "break value" of a process.

Syntax

```
#include <malloc.h>
void *sbrk(int change);
int change;     Number of bytes by which the break value is to be changed
```

Example Call

```
buffer = (char *) sbrk(80); /* Allocate an 80-byte buffer */
```

Returns

The return value from *sbrk* is the address of the previous break value. If *sbrk* fails, it returns −1.

See Also

brk, free, malloc

---

stackavail ◀

Purpose

Use *stackavail* before calling *alloca* to determine the approximate size in bytes of the space available on the stack for allocation.

Syntax

```
#include <malloc.h>
size_t stackavail(void);
```

Example Call

```
room_in_stack = stackavail();
```

Returns

The *stackavail* function returns the approximate number of bytes available on the stack.

See Also

alloca

Example 5-1   Illustrate the use of the memory allocation routines by allocating two buffers, one with *calloc* and the other by *malloc*. Enlarge one of the buffers by calling *realloc*. Free the buffers using *free*.

```
 1:  #include <stdio.h>
 2:  #include <stdlib.h>
 3:
 4:  main()
 5:  {
 6:      unsigned char *buffer1, *buffer2;
 7:
 8:  /* Allocate room for string and check for NULL */
 9:      if ((buffer1 = (char *) calloc(100, 80)) == NULL)
10:      {
11:          printf("calloc Failed.\n");
12:          exit(1);
13:      }
14:      printf("Buffer allocated by calloc."
15:             "Enter string to store: ");
16:      gets(buffer1);
17:      printf("\nYou entered: %s\n",buffer1);
18:
19:  /* Now allocate another buffer using malloc */
20:      if( (buffer2 = (char *)malloc(10)) == NULL )
21:      {
22:          printf("malloc Failed.\n");
23:          exit(1);
24:      }
25:      printf("Buffer allocated by malloc."
26:             "Enter another string to store: ");
27:      gets(buffer2);
28:      printf("\nYou entered: %s\n",buffer2);
29:  /* Now enlarge size of buffer and redisplay string */
30:      if( (buffer2 = (char *)realloc((void *)buffer2, 80))
31:          == NULL )
32:      {
33:          printf("Reallocation Failed.\n");
34:          exit(1);
35:      }
36:      printf("Buffer still contains: %s\n",buffer2);
37:  /* Free the buffers */
38:      free(buffer1);
39:      free(buffer2);
40:  }
```

6

Buffer Manipulation

The buffer manipulation routines manipulate chunks of bytes in memory. They allow you to copy data from one area of memory to another, initialize a block of memory, compare the contents of two buffers, and search for the occurrence of a specific character (actually, this can be any value that fits into a byte) in a buffer. These routines are helpful, for example, when you are directly copying a screenful of text (or image) from a buffer to the video memory. Another interesting example of using the buffer manipulation routines would be in a file comparison utility. Provided you have enough memory, you could copy two files into memory and use a routine such as *memcmp* to see if the files match. The buffer manipulation routines are declared in the header files *memory.h* and *string.h*.

► memccpy, memcpy

Purpose

Use *memcpy* to copy *count* bytes from the buffer at address *source* to another buffer at *dest*. The *memccpy* function works similarly, but it stops copying once the character *c* is copied to *dest*.

Syntax

```
#include <memory.h>  or  #include <string.h>
void *memccpy(void *dest, void *source, int c,  unsigned
                                                     count);
void *memcpy(void *dest, const void *source, size_t count);
void      *dest;       Pointer to buffer to which data will be copied
void   *source;        Pointer to buffer from which data will be copied
                       (const for memcpy)
int       c;           Last character to be copied by memccpy
unsigned  count;       Maximum number of bytes to be copied (type is
                       size__t for memcpy)
```

Example Call

```
memcpy(dest, src, 80); /* Copy 80 bytes from dest to src */
```

Returns

The *memcpy* function returns a pointer to the destination buffer *dest*. For *memccpy*, if *c* was copied, the return value is a pointer to the character following *c* in *dest*. Otherwise, *memccpy* returns NULL.

See Also

```
memmove, strcpy, strncpy
```

► memchr

Purpose

Use the *memchr* function to search through the first *count* bytes in the buffer at the address *buffer* and find the first occurrence of the character *c*.

Syntax

```
#include <memory.h>   or  #include <string.h>
void *memchr(const void *buffer, int c, size_t count);
const void *buffer;        Pointer to buffer in which search takes place
```

memchr

```
int        c;            Character to look for
size_t     count;        Maximum number of bytes to be examined
```

Example Call

```
/*Look for the first occurrence of 'I' in a 100 byte buffer*/
first_i = memchr(start_address, 'I', 100);
```

Returns

If *memchr* finds the character *c*, it returns a pointer to this character in *buffer*. Otherwise, *memchr* returns a NULL.

See Also

memcmp, strchr

---

memcmp, memicmp ◀

Purpose

Use *memcmp* to compare the first *count* bytes of the two buffers *buffer1* and *buffer2*. Use *memicmp* for comparing the buffers without regard to case of the letters.

Syntax

```
#include <memory.h>  or  #include <string.h>
int memcmp(const void *buffer1, const void *buffer2,
           size_t count);
int memicmp(void *buffer1, void *buffer2, unsigned count);
const void *buffer1;    Pointer to first buffer (no const for memicmp)
const void *buffer2;    Pointer to second buffer (no const for
                        memicmp)
size_t count;           Number of bytes to be compared (type is
                        unsigned for memicmp)
```

Example Call

```
if (memcmp(buffer1, buffer2, sizeof(buffer1)) == 0)
           printf("The buffers are identical\n");
```

Returns

Each function returns an integer less than, equal to, or greater than 0 accordingly as the string *buffer1* is less than, equal to, or greater than the string *buffer2*.

See Also

strcmp, strncmp

► memmove

Purpose

Use *memmove* to copy *count* bytes from the buffer at address *source* to another buffer at *dest*. Parts of the source and destination buffers may overlap.

Syntax

```
#include <string.h>
void *memmove(void *dest, const void *source, size_t count);
void      *dest;        Pointer to buffer to which data will be copied
const void *source;     Pointer to buffer from which data will be copied
size_t     count;       Maximum number of bytes to be copied
```

Example Call

```
memmove(dest, src, sizeof(src));
```

Returns

The *memmove* function returns a pointer to the destination buffer *dest*.

See Also

memcpy, movedata

► memset

Purpose

Use the *memset* function to set the first *count* bytes in the *buffer* to the character *c*.

Syntax

```
#include <memory.h>   or  #include <string.h>
void *memset(void *buffer, int c, size_t count);
void      *buffer;     Pointer to memory where bytes are to be set
int        c;          Each byte in buffer will be set to this character
size_t     count;      Maximum number of bytes to be set
```

Example Call

```
memset(big_buffer, '\0', 2048);
```

Returns

The *memset* function returns the argument *buffer*.

memset

See Also

memcpy, memmove, strcpy, strncpy

Example

Line 9 in Example 6-1 uses *memset* to initialize a large buffer.

movedata

Purpose

Use *movedata* to copy *count* bytes from a source address to a destination address. This function is useful for moving data between different segments.

Syntax

```
#include <memory.h>   or  #include <string.h>
void movedata(unsigned srcseg, unsigned srcoff, unsigned
                                                dstseg,
          unsigned dstoff, unsigned count);
```

unsigned srcseg;	*Segment address of source*
unsigned srcoff;	*Offset of source address*
unsigned dstseg;	*Segment address of destination*
unsigned dstoff;	*Offset of destination address*
unsigned count;	*Number of bytes to be copied*

Example Call

movedata(0xf000, 0xe000, bufseg, bufoff, 32);

See Also

memcpy, memmove

Example

Line 16 in Example 6-1 shows how *movedata* is used to copy a buffer directly to the display memory.

swab

Purpose

Use *swab* to copy *count* bytes from the buffer at address *source* to another buffer at *dest* after swapping adjacent even- and odd-numbered bytes.

Syntax

```
#include <stdlib.h>
```

```
void swab(char *source, char *dest, int count);
void      *source;    Pointer to buffer from which data will be copied
void      *dest;      Pointer to buffer to which data will be copied
int        count;     Number of bytes to be copied
```

Example Call

```
swab(src, dest, 16);
```

See Also

```
_lrotl, _lrotr, _rotl, _rotr
```

Example 6-1   In a Color Graphics Adapter (and EGA in text mode), the video memory starts at the address B800:0000. Prepare a buffer with 2000 (25 rows by 80 columns) short integers. Initialize the entire buffer to 0 (use *memset*). Now copy the contents of the buffer into video memory using *movedata*. The effect of setting the video memory to 0 is to clear the display screen. This approach can be used for preparing text output off screen and for updating the display very rapidly.

```
 1:#include <dos.h>
 2:#include <memory.h>
 3:static short dispbuf[25][80]; /* Display buffer */
 4:main()
 5:{
 6:    void far *address;
 7:    unsigned bufseg, bufoff;
 8:/* Initialize display buffer to zero */
 9:    memset(dispbuf, '\0', sizeof(dispbuf));
10:/* Get segment and offset address of buffer */
11:    address = (void far *)dispbuf;
12:    bufseg = FP_SEG(address);
13:    bufoff = FP_OFF(address);
14:/* Copy buffer into video memory -- clears screen */
15:/* Change 0xb800 to 0xb000 for monochrome adapter */
16:    movedata( bufseg, bufoff, 0xb800, 0x0000,
17:              sizeof(dispbuf));
18:}
```

III

Microsoft C Data Processing

7

Data Conversion

Information management with computers frequently requires crunching numbers. These numbers are internally represented in several forms depending on the type of C variable in which the value is held. The Microsoft C data conversion routines, declared in the header file *stdlib.h*, allow us to convert back and forth between the internal form of a C variable and the character string representations that we can read.

► atof

Purpose

Use the *atof* function to convert the argument *string* into a double value.

Syntax

```
#include <stdlib.h>   or   #include <math.h>
double atof(const char *string);
const char *string;      String to be converted
```

Example Call

```
dbl_value = atof("7.25 percent"); /* dbl_value = 7.25 */
```

Returns

The *atof* function returns the double precision value after conversion.

See Also

```
atoi, atol, strtod
```

► atoi, atol

Purpose

Use the *atoi* and *atol* functions to convert the argument *string* into an *int* and a *long* value, respectively.

Syntax

```
#include <stdlib.h>
int atoi(const char *string);
int atol(const char *string);
const char *string;      String to be converted
```

Example Call

```
int_value = atoi("250 pages");   /* int_value = 250 */
long_value = atol("20165000 bytes");   /* long_value = 20165000
                                                            */
```

Returns

These functions return the converted value.

atoi, atol

See Also

atof, strtol, strtoul

---

ecvt, fcvt ◄

Purpose

Use *ecvt* to convert *value* into a null-terminated character string with *count* digits. After return from *ecvt*, if *dec* is 0 or negative, the decimal point lies at the beginning of the string or to the left of the first digit. If *sign* is 0, the number is positive; otherwise, it is negative. The *fcvt* function is similar to *ecvt* but *fcvt* rounds *value* to *count* digits.

Syntax

```
#include <stdlib.h>
char *ecvt(double value, int count, int *dec, int *sign);
char *gcvt(double value, int count, int *dec, int *sign);
double value;     Floating-point value to be converted to string
int    count;     Number of digits to be stored
int    *dec;      Pointer to integer where position of decimal point will be
                  returned
int    *sign;     Pointer to integer where sign of the number is returned
```

Example Call

```
printf("Result = %s\n", ecvt(result, 6, &d_position, &sign));
```

Returns

Each function returns a pointer to an internal static buffer where the string of digits is stored. The next call to either *ecvt* or *fcvt* will destroy the result.

See Also

atof, gcvt

---

gcvt ◄

Purpose

Use *gcvt* to convert a floating-point value to a character string. Unlike *ecvt* and *fcvt*, *gcvt* returns the result in a character buffer supplied by you.

Syntax

```
#include <stdlib.h>
```

```
char *gcvt(double value, int digits, char *buffer);
double value;        Floating point value to be converted to string
int    digits;       Number of significant digits to be stored
char   *buffer;      Pointer to character array where result is returned
```

Example Call

```
gcvt(value, significant_digits, result_string);
```

Returns

The *gcvt* function returns the argument *buffer*.

See Also

atof, ecvt, fcvt

► itoa, ltoa, ultoa

Purpose

Use *itoa* to convert an *int* value to a null-terminated character string. The *ltoa* and *ultoa* functions are for converting *long* and *unsigned long* values, respectively.

Syntax

```
#include <stdlib.h>
char *itoa(int ivalue, char *string, int radix);
char *ltoa(long lvalue, char *string, int radix);
char *ultoa(unsigned long ulvalue, char *string, int radix);
int             ivalue;      Integer value to be converted to string by itoa
long            lvalue;      Long integer value to be converted to string
                             by ltoa
unsigned long ulvalue;       Unsigned long integer value to be converted
                             to string by ultoa
char    *string;             Pointer to character array where result is
                             returned
int     radix;               Radix in which the result is expressed (in the
                             range 2 to 36)
```

Example Call

```
itoa(32, buffer, 16); /* buffer will contain "20" */
ltoa(0x10000, string, 10);  /* string = "65536"  */
ultoa(0x100000, string, 10); /* string = "131072" */
```

Returns

Each function returns the argument *string*.

itoa, ltoa, ultoa

See Also

atoi, atol

---

strtod ◄

Purpose

Use the *strtod* function to convert *string* to a double precision value. The string is expected to be of the form:

```
[whitespace][sign][digits.digits]
                              [exponent_letter][sign][digits]
```

where *whitespace* refers to (optional) blanks and tab characters, *sign* is a + or a −, and the *digits* are decimal digits. The *exponent _letter* can be any one of d, D, e, or E (no matter which exponent letter is used, the exponent always denotes a power of 10).

Syntax

```
double strtod(const char *string, char **endptr);
const char  *string;       Pointer to character array from which double
                           precision value will be extracted
char    **endptr;          On return points to character in string where
                           conversion stopped provided the argument is
                           not NULL
```

Example Call

```
dbl_value = strtod(input_string, &endptr);
```

Returns

The *strtod* function returns the double precision value.

See Also

atof, strtol, strtoul

---

strtol, strtoul ◄

Purpose

Use the *strtol* function to convert *string* to a long integer value. Use *strtoul* when you want to convert to an unsigned long integer. The input string is expected to be of the form:

```
[whitespace][sign][0][x or X][digits]
```

where *whitespace* refers to (optional) blanks and tab characters, *sign* is a + or a −, and the *digits* are decimal digits. The string is expected to contain a representation of the long integer using the argument *radix* as the base of the number system. However, if *radix* is given as 0, these functions will use the first character in the *string* to determine the radix of the value. The rules are shown in Table 7-1.

Table 7-1. Rules for Finding Radix

First Character	Next Character	Radix Selected
0	0–7	Radix 8 is used (i.e., octal digits expected)
0	x or X	Radix 16 (i.e., hexadecimal digits expected)
1–9	—	Radix 10 (decimal digits expected)

Syntax

```
long strtol(const char *string, char **endptr, int radix);
unsigned long strtoul(const char *string, char **endptr,
                      int radix);
```

`const char *string;`	*Pointer to character array from which the value will be extracted*
`char **endptr;`	*On return points to character in* string *where conversion stopped (provided the argument is not NULL)*
`int radix;`	*Radix in which the value is expressed in the* string *(radix must be in the range 2 to 36)*

Example Call

```
value = strtol(input, &endptr, radix);
```

Returns

Each function returns the converted value.

See Also

`atol, strtoul`

Example

Example 7-1 shows a hexadecimal calculator program that uses *strtoul* to read hexadecimal values from the command-line arguments (lines 14 and 15).

Example 7-1   This example shows a hexadecimal calculator designed to be invoked with the command line *calc operand_1 operation operand_2*, where *calc* is the name of the program, *operation* is one of +, −, *, or /, and *operand_1* and *operand_2* are the hexadecimal operands. The program uses *strtoul* to read the operands.

```
1:#include <stdio.h>
```

strtol, strtoul

```
 2:#include <stdlib.h>
 3:
 4:static char command[80] = " ";
 5:
 6:main(int argc, char **argv)
 7:{
 8:    unsigned long op1, op2;
 9:    if(argc < 4)
10:    {
11:        printf("Usage: %s <operand1> <operation> "
12:                "<operand2>\n", argv[0]);
13:    }
14:    op1 = strtoul(argv[1], (char **)NULL, 16);
15:    op2 = strtoul(argv[3], (char **)NULL, 16);
16:
17:    switch (argv[2][0])
18:    {
19:        case '+':
20:            printf("%lX (hex)\n", op1 + op2);
21:            break;
22:        case '-':
23:            printf("%lX (hex)\n", op1 - op2);
24:            break;
25:        case '*':
26:            printf("%lX (hex)\n", op1 * op2);
27:            break;
28:        case '/':
29:            if(op2 == 0L)
30:            {
31:                printf("Can't divide by zero!\n");
32:            }
33:            else
34:                printf("%lX (hex)\n", op1 / op2);
35:            break;
36:    }
37:}
```

8
Math Functions

In addition to the support for basic floating-point operations in the language, the Microsoft C library also includes a set of functions, the math functions, to compute common mathematical functions such as the sine and the cosine. These routines are declared in the header files *math.h*, *float.h*, and *stdlib.h*.

Note that two types of errors can occur in the math functions. A "domain" error occurs when the arguments to a function are outside the domain of values for which that function is defined. When this error occurs, the global error indicator *errno* (defined in *errno.h*) will be set to the constant EDOM. A "range" error occurs when the result of a math function cannot be represented as a *double* value. If the result is large so that there is an overflow, the function returns the constant HUGE_VAL (defined in *float.h*) and sets *errno* to ERANGE. If the value is too small (causing an underflow), the function returns 0.

► abs, fabs, labs

Purpose

Use *abs*, *fabs*, and *labs* to get the absolute value of an integer, a floating-point variable, and a long integer, respectively.

Syntax

```
#include <stdlib.h>      For abs and labs
#include <math.h>        For fabs
int    abs(int ivalue);
double fabs(double dvalue);
long   labs(long lvalue);
int    ivalue;           Integer whose absolute value is returned by abs
double dvalue;           Floating-point value whose magnitude is
                         returned by fabs
int    lvalue;           Integer whose absolute value is returned by labs
```

Example Call

```
x = abs(-5);             /* x will be 5 now      */
y = fabs(-5.15);         /* y will be 5.15       */
lresult = labs(-65540L); /* result will be 65540 */
```

Returns

Each function returns the absolute value of the argument.

See Also

cabs, hypot

► acos, asin, atan

Purpose

Use *acos*, *asin*, and *atan* to compute the arc cosine, arc sine, and arc tangent of an argument *x*. For *acos* and *asin*, *x* must lie in the range −1 to 1. Otherwise, a domain error occurs.

Syntax

```
#include <math.h>
double acos(double x);
double asin(double x);
double atan(double x);
double x;        Argument whose arc cosine, arc sine, or arc tangent is to be
                 computed
```

acos, asin, atan

Example Call

```
angle = acos(0.5);   /* angle is "pi"/3         */
angle = asin(0.707)  /* angle is roughly "pi"/4 */
angle = atan(1.0)    /* angle is "pi"/4         */
```

Returns

An angle in radians is returned.

See Also

```
atan2, cos, sin, tan
```

atan2

Purpose

Use the *atan2* function to compute the arc tangent of the ratio of the arguments y/x. The result will be an angle with value between $-\pi$ and π radians. It uses the sign of the two arguments to determine the quadrant in which the angle should lie.

Syntax

```
#include <math.h>
double atan2(double y, double x);
double x, y;    Arctangent of y/x will be computed
```

Example Call

```
angle = atan2(y, x);
```

Returns

Provided both arguments x and y are nonzero, *atan2* returns an angle whose tangent is equal to x. However, if both arguments are zero, a domain error occurs.

See Also

```
atan, tan
```

cabs

Purpose

Use *cabs* to compute the magnitude of a complex number z stored in a *complex* structure, which is defined in *math.h* as:

```
struct complex
```

```
{
    double x;    /* Real part of the complex number      */
    double y;    /* Imaginary part of the complex number */
};
```

Syntax

```
#include <math.h>
double cabs(struct complex z);
struct complex  z;      Structure containing the complex whose magitude
                        is computed
```

Example Call

```
magnitude = cabs(z);
```

Returns

If the magnitude of *z* is too large, a range error occurs. Otherwise, *cabs* returns the magnitude of the complex number.

See Also

abs, fabs, labs, hypot

► ceil, floor

Purpose

Use the *ceil* function to find the smallest integer that is greater than or equal to *x*. The *floor* function returns the largest integer that is less than or equal to *x*.

Syntax

```
#include <math.h>
double ceil(double x);
double floor(double x);
double x;      Value whose "ceiling" or "floor" is to be returned
```

Example Call

```
x_ceiling = ceil(4.15);   /* x_ceiling will be 5.0 */
x_floor = floor(4.15);    /* x_floor will be 4.0   */
```

Returns

The functions return the floor or the ceiling of *x* as appropriate.

See Also

modf

ceil, floor

__clear87, __control87, __status87 ◀

Purpose

Use _clear87 to retrieve and reset to 0 the floating-point status word, which is a combination of the 8087 math coprocessor's status word and other conditions detected by the 8087 exception handler. The _status87 function lets you get the current contents of this status word. The _control87 is used to get and set the floating-point control word. See *The Waite Group's Microsoft C Bible* for further details about these functions and their arguments.

Syntax

```
#include <float.h>
unsigned int _clear87(void);
unsigned int _control87(unsigned new, unsigned mask);
unsigned int _status87(void);
unsigned int new;      New control word bit values
unsigned int mask;     Mask to indicate which bits of control word to set
```

Example Call

```
status = _clear87();
status = _control87(PC_24, MCW_PC); /* 24-bit precision */
if(_status87() & SW_ZERODIVIDE) puts("Zero divide error");
```

Returns

The _clear87 function returns the prior contents of the floating-point status word, while _status87 returns the current contents. The _control87 function returns the floating-point control word.

See Also

_fpreset, matherr

cos, sin, tan ◀

Purpose

Use *cos*, *sin*, and *tan* to compute the cosine, sine, and tangent of the angle *x* (in radians), respectively.

Syntax

```
#include <math.h>
double cos(double x);
```

```
double sin(double x);
double tan(double x);
double x;      Angle in radians whose cosine, sine, or tangent is to be
               computed
```

Example Call

```
cos_x = cos(0.0);  /* cos_x will be 1.0 */
```

Returns

The functions return the cosine, sine, or tangent of x as appropriate. If value of x is large in magnitude, the result of *cos* and *sin* may be very imprecise.

See Also

```
acos, asin, atan, atan2
```

Example

Example 8-1 computes the cosine, sine, and tangent of angles between 0 and 180°.

► cosh, sinh, tanh

Purpose

Use *cosh*, *sinh*, and *tanh* to compute the hyperbolic cosine, hyperbolic sine, and hyperbolic tangent of x, respectively.

Syntax

```
#include <math.h>
double cosh(double x);
double sinh(double x);
double tanh(double x);
double x;      Argument whose hyperbolic cosine, hyperbolic sine, or
               hyperbolic tangent is to be computed
```

Example Call

```
result = cosh(x);
```

Returns

Each function returns the hyperbolic cosine, hyperbolic sine, or hyperbolic tangent of x as appropriate. For *cosh* and *sinh*, a range error will occur if the result is too large (a *double* variable can be as large as 10^{308}).

See Also

```
cos, sin, tan
```

dieeetomsbin, dmsbintoieee, ◀
fieeetomsbin, fmsbintoieee

Purpose

Use the *dieeetomsbin* and *dmsbintoieee* functions to convert a double precision number from IEEE format to Microsoft binary format and back again. Use *fieeetomsbin* and *fmsbintoieee* for converting single precision values. The Microsoft binary format is used by Microsoft BASIC to store floating-point numbers.

Syntax

```
#include <math.h>
int dieeetomsbin(double *src8, double *dst8);
int dmsbintoieee(double *src8, double *dst8);
int fieeetomsbin(float *src4, float *dst4);
int fmsbintoieee(float *src4, float *dst4);
```
double *src8;   *Pointer to double variable to be converted by*
                 dieeetomsbin *or* dmsbintoieee
double *dst8;   *Pointer to double variable where* dieeetomsbin *or*
                 dmsbintoieee *will return the result*
float *src4;   *Pointer to floating variable to be converted by*
                 fieeetomsbin *or* fmsbintoieee
float *dst4;   *Pointer to floating variable where* fieeetomsbin *or*
                 fmsbintoieee *will return the result*

Example Call

```
dieeetomsbin(&d_ieee, &d_msbin);
```

Returns

These functions will return 0 if the conversion is successful and 1 if conversion caused an overflow.

div, ldiv ◀

Purpose

Use the *div* function to divide the first integer *numer* by the second one *denom* and obtain the resulting quotient and remainder packed in a structure of type *div_t*. The structure of type *div_t* is defined in *stdlib.h* as:

```
typedef struct
{
    int quot;    /* The quotient */
    int rem;     /* The remainder */
```

```
} div_t;
```

The *ldiv* routine provides the same function for long integers. The *ldiv_t* structure is similar to *div_t* except that each member is a *long* instead of an *int*.

Syntax

```
#include <stdlib.h>
ldiv_t ldiv(long lnumer, long ldenom);
div_t div(int inumer, int idenom);
int  inumer;        Numerator for div
int  idenom;        Denominator for div
long lnumer;        Numerator for ldiv
long ldenom;        Denominator for ldiv
```

Example Call

```
result = div(32, 5);              /* result.quot = 6 and
                                             result.rem = 2 */
lresult = ldiv(65540L, 65536L); /* lresult.quot = 1,
                                          lresult.rem = 4 */
```

Returns

Each function returns the appropriate structure containing the quotient and remainder of the division.

See Also

```
fmod
```

▶ exp

Purpose

Use *exp* to compute the exponential of the *double* variable *x*. The exponential of a variable *x* is e^x where *e* is the base of natural logarithm ($e = 2.7182818$).

Syntax

```
#include <math.h>
double exp(double x);
double x;        Variable whose exponential is to be computed
```

Example Call

```
y = exp(x);
```

Returns

Normally, *exp* returns the exponential of *x*. If the result is too large, a range error occurs.

exp

See Also

log, log10

fmod

Purpose

Use the *fmod* function to compute the floating-point remainder after dividing the floating-point number *x* by *y* and ensuring that the quotient is the largest possible integer.

Syntax

```
#include <math.h>
double fmod(double x, double y);
double x, y;        The remainder after the division x/y is returned
```

Example Call

```
rem = fmod(24.95, 5.5); /* rem will be 2.95 */
```

Returns

The *fmod* function returns the remainder of the division.

See Also

floor

__fpreset ◄

Purpose

Use *_fpreset* to reinitialize the floating-point math package. This function is provided so that you can begin with a clean floating-point system after using functions such as *system*, *signal*, and the spawn family of functions.

Syntax

```
void _fpreset(void);
```

Example Call

```
_fpreset();
```

See Also

_clear87, _control87, signal, _status87

► frexp, ldexp

Purpose

Use *frexp* to break down the floating-point number x into a mantissa m, whose absolute value lies between 0.5 and 1.0, and an integer exponent n, so that $x = m\ 2^n$. If x is 0, the exponent will also be 0. The *ldexp* function performs the reverse operation. It computes *mantissa* times 2^{exp}.

Syntax

```
#include <math.h>
double frexp(double x, int *expptr);
double ldexp(double mantissa, int exp);
double x;            Floating-point argument to be decomposed by frexp
int    *expptr;      Pointer to an integer where frexp returns the
                     exponent
double mantissa;     Floating-point value of the mantissa for ldexp
int    exp;          Integer exponent for ldexp
```

Example Call

```
mantissa = frexp(5.1, &exponent);
/* mantissa will be 0.6375, exponent = 3      */
value = ldexp(0.6375, 3); /* value will be 5.1 */
```

Returns

The *frexp* function returns the mantissa m computed as already described. The *ldexp* function returns the value x times 2^{exp}.

See Also

modf

► hypot

Purpose

Use *hypot* to compute the length of the hypotenuse of a right triangle, given the length of the two sides.

Syntax

```
#include <math.h>
double hypot(double x, double y);
double x, y;    sqrt(x*x + y*y) will be returned
```

Example Call

```
length = hypot(3.0, 4.0); /* length = 5.0 */
```

hypot

Returns

The normal return value is the length of the hypotenuse as already described. If the result is too large, a range error occurs.

See Also

cabs

j0, j1, jn, y0, y1, yn ◀

Purpose

Use the functions in this group to evaluate Bessel functions of first and second kind of any integer order for an argument (for further details, see a reference book such as *Handbook of Mathematical Functions* by M. Abramowitz and I. A. Stegun, Dover, 1970).

Syntax

```
#include <math.h>
double j0(double x);
double j1(double x);
double jn(int n, double x);
double y0(double x);
double y1(double x);
double yn(int n, double x);
double x;      Positive argument for the Bessel function
int    n;      Integer order of the Bessel function for jn and yn
```

Example Call

```
z = jn(2,x);
```

Returns

Normally, the functions return the value of the appropriate Bessel function at the specified argument *x* and for the order *n* in the case of *jn* and *yn*. However, if the Bessel functions of the second kind are called with a negative *x*, a domain error occurs.

log, log10 ◀

Purpose

Use *log* and *log10*, respectively, to compute the natural logarithm and logarithm to the base 10 of the positive *double* variable *x*.

Syntax

```
#include <math.h>
double log(double x);
double log10(double x);
double x;        Variable whose logarithm is to be computed
```

Example Call

```
y = log(2);    /* y = 0.693147 */
a = log10(2);  /* a = 0.30103  */
```

Returns

For positive *x*, *log* and *log10* return the logarithm of *x*. If *x* is negative, a domain error occurs. If *x* is 0, a range error occurs.

See Also

```
exp, pow
```

▶ __lrotl, __lrotr, __rotl, __rotr

Purpose

Use *__lrotl* and *__lrotr* to rotate the bits in an unsigned long integer variable to the left and to the right, respectively. The corresponding functions for unsigned integers are *__rotl* and *__rotr*.

Syntax

```
#include <stdlib.h>
unsigned long int _lrotl(unsigned long lvalue, int shift);
unsigned long int _lrotr(unsigned long lvalue, int shift);
unsigned _rotr(unsigned value, int shift);
unsigned _rotl(unsigned value, int shift);
unsigned long lvalue;    Value to be rotated by __lrotl or __lrotr
unsigned int  ivalue;    Value to be rotated by __rotl or __rotr
int           shift;     Number of bits to shift
```

Sample

```
result = _lrotl(0x012345467L, 4);   /* result is 0x12345670 */
result = _lrotr(0x012345467L, 16);  /* result is 0x45670123 */
result = _rotl(0x1234, 8);          /* result is 3412h      */
result = _rotr(0x1234, 4);          /* result is 4123h      */
```

Returns

Each function returns the value after rotation.

__lrotl, __lrotr, __rotl, __rotr

matherr ◀

Purpose

The default *matherr* function is called by a math function whenever an error occurs. You can provide your own copy of *matherr* to customize error handling. The *matherr* function is always called with the pointer to an *exception* structure, which is defined in *math.h* as follows:

```
struct exception
{
    int type;        /* exception type - see Microsoft C Ref. */
    char *name;      /* name of function where error occurred */
    double arg1;     /* first argument to function            */
    double arg2;     /* second argument (if any) to function  */
    double retval;   /* value to be returned by function      */
} ;
```

The value put into the field *retval* by *matherr* will be returned by the math function to its calling process.

Syntax

```
#include <math.h>
int matherr(struct exception *error_info);
struct exception *error_info;        Pointer to a structure that contains
                                     information about the error that
                                     just occurred
```

Returns

The *matherr* function should return a zero to indicate an error and a nonzero value to indicate successful corrective action. The math function that called *matherr* will display an error message and set *errno* to an appropriate value if *matherr* returns a zero. Keep this in mind when writing your own *matherr* function.

modf ◀

Purpose

Use the *modf* function to separate the floating-point number *x* into its fractional part and its integral part.

Syntax

```
#include <math.h>
double modf(double x, double *intptr);
double x;          Floating-point value to be decomposed
double *intptr;    Integer part of x is returned at this location
```

modf

Example Call

```
fraction = modf(24.95, &int_part); /* fraction is .95 */
```

Returns

The *modf* function returns the signed fractional part of *x*.

See Also

```
frexp, ldexp
```

---

pow

Purpose

The *pow* function computes the value of *x* raised to the power *y*. The arguments *x* and *y* both must not be 0, and when *x* is negative, *y* must be an integer.

Syntax

```
#include <math.h>
double pow(double x, double y);
double x, y;      x raised to the power y will be computed by pow
```

Example Call

```
x = pow(2.0, 3.0); /* x will be 8.0    */
```

Returns

When both *x* and *y* are nonzero positive numbers, *pow* returns the value *x* raised to the power *y*. If *x* is nonzero and *y* is zero, the return value is 1.

See Also

```
log, log10, sqrt
```

▶ rand, srand

Purpose

The *rand* function generates a pseudorandom integer with value between 0 and the constant RAND_MAX (defined to be 32,767 in *stdlib.h*). Use *srand* to set *seed* as the starting point for the pseudorandom integers generated by *rand*. If *seed* is 1, the random number generator is initialized to its default starting point.

Syntax

```
#include <stdlib.h>
int rand(void);
void srand(unsigned seed);
unsigned seed;      Starting seed for srand
```

Example Call

```
random_value = rand();
srand(new_seed);
```

Returns

The *rand* function returns the pseudorandom integer it generated.

Example

Example 8-2 shows how these routines are used.

---

sqrt ◀

Purpose

Use *sqrt* to compute the square root of a nonnegative *double* variable *x*.

Syntax

```
#include <math.h>
double sqrt(double x);
double x;     Variable whose square root is to be computed
```

Example Call

```
sqrt_2 = sqrt(2.0); /* sqrt_2 = 1.414 */
```

Returns

The *sqrt* function returns the square root of *x*. However, if *x* is negative, a domain error occurs.

See Also

pow

Example 8-1 This program prints a table showing the cosines, sines, and tangents of the angles between 0 and 180° in steps of 10°.

```
1:/* Print a table of cosines, sines, and tangents  */
2:#include <stdio.h>
3:#include <stddef.h>      /* errno is declared here */
4:#include <errno.h> /* error constants defined here*/
```

```
 5:#include <math.h>
 6:#define  R_TO_D    57.29578 /* radians to degrees  */
 7:main()
 8:{
 9:    double angle, radians, cresult, sresult, tresult;
10:
11:    printf("Angle\t\tCosine\t\tSine\t\tTan\n");
12:    for(angle = 0.0; angle <= 180.0; angle += 10.0)
13:    {
14:        radians = angle / R_TO_D;
15:        cresult = cos(radians);
16:        sresult = sin(radians);
17:        tresult = tan(radians);
18:        if(errno != ERANGE)
19:        {
20:            printf("%f deg.\t%f\t%f\t%f\n",
21:            angle, cresult, sresult, tresult);
22:        }
23:    }
24:}
```

Example 8-2   This example uses *rand* and *srand* to generate a random sequence of the numbers between 1 and 20. This means that the sequence must contain only the numbers 1 through 20 in a random order with no number appearing more than once. You can use such a random sequence to assign tasks among workers in a group.

```
 1:
 2:/* Generate random sequence of random numbers */
 3:#include <stdio.h>
 4:#include <stdlib.h>
 5:#include <time.h>      /* time() used for random seed */
 6:#define MAXNUM 20      /* maximum number in sequence  */
 7:main()
 8:{
 9:    int seq[20], count=0, i, randnum;
10:/* Initialize the random number generator */
11:    srand((unsigned)time(NULL));
12:    while(count < 20)
13:    {
14:        randnum = (rand() % MAXNUM) + 1;
15:/* Is this number already present in seq[] */
16:        for(i=0; i<count; i++)
17:        {
18:            if(randnum == seq[i]) break;
19:        }
20:        if(i>=count)    /* Not in seq[] */
21:        {
22:            seq[count] = randnum;
23:            count++;
```

```
24:            }
25:        }
26:/* Print the random sequence */
27:    printf("Random sequence (1-%d) = \n", MAXNUM);
28:    for(i=0; i<count; i++) printf("%d ", seq[i]);
29:    printf("\n");
30:}
```

9

Character Classification and Conversion

Microsoft C provides a set of macros, defined in the header file *ctype.h*, that are useful for classifying and converting characters. This chapter summarizes the macros.

► isalnum

Purpose

Use the *isalnum* macro to check if the character *c* is alphanumeric. It is equivalent to testing if *isalpha* or *isdigit* is true for *c*.

Syntax

```
#include <ctype.h>
int isalnum(int c);
int c;      Character being tested
```

Example Call

```
if(isalnum(c) != 0) printf("%c is alphanumeric\n", c);
```

Returns

The *isalnum* macro returns a nonzero value if the *c* is indeed an alphanumeric character. Otherwise, it returns a zero.

See Also

```
isalpha, isdigit
```

► isalpha

Purpose

Use *isalpha* macro to check if the character *c* is either a lowercase or an uppercase letter.

Syntax

```
#include <ctype.h>
int isalpha(int c);
int c;      Character being tested
```

Example Call

```
if(isalpha(c) != 0) printf("%c is letter\n", c);
```

Returns

The *isalpha* macro returns a nonzero value if *c* is a letter. Otherwise, it returns a zero.

See Also

```
islower, isupper
```

isalpha

isascii ◄

Purpose

Use *isascii* macro to check if an arbitrary integer value is a valid ASCII character.

Syntax

```
#include <ctype.h>
int isascii(int c);
int c;      Integer value being checked
```

Example Call

```
if(isascii(c) == 0) printf("%d <- not ASCII value\n", c);
```

Returns

The *isascii* macro returns a nonzero value if the *c* is indeed a valid ASCII character. Otherwise, it returns a zero.

See Also

toascii

iscntrl, isdigit, isgraph, islower, isprint, ◄
ispunct, isspace, isupper, isxdigit

Purpose

Use this group of macros to check for specific properties of the character *c* such as whether it is a control character, a digit, lowercase, or printable. Table 9-1 shows the test performed by each of the macros.

Table 9-1. Character Classification Tests

Macro Name	Tests for
iscntrl	Control character
isdigit	Decimal digit
isgraph	Printable character excluding the space
islower	Lowercase letter
isprint	Printable character including space
ispunct	Punctuation character
isspace	"Whitespace" character (space; formfeed, \f; newline, \n; carriage return, \r; horizontal tab, \t; and vertical tab, \v)

Table 9-1. (cont.)

Macro Name	Tests for
isupper	uppercase letter
isxdigit	Hexadecimal digit

Syntax

```
#include <ctype.h>
int iscntrl(int c);
int isdigit(int c);
int isgraph(int c);
int islower(int c);
int isprint(int c);
int ispunct(int c);
int isspace(int c);
int isupper(int c);
int isxdigit(int c);
int c;     Character to be tested
```

Example Call

```
if(isprint(c) != 0) printf("%c is printable\n", c);
if(isdigit(c) != 0) printf("%c is a digit\n", c);
if(iscntrl(c) != 0) printf("%d is a control char\n", c);
```

Returns

Each macro returns a nonzero value if the *c* satisfies the criterion for that macro. Otherwise, it returns a zero.

See Also

```
isalnum, isalpha, isascii
```

---

 toascii

Purpose

Use *toascii* macro to convert *c* to a valid ASCII character by setting its eighth bit to 0.

Syntax

```
int toascii(int c);
int c;     Integer to be converted to ASCII
```

Example Call

```
c = toascii(0xc1);  /*c will be 'A' whose ASCII code is 0x41*/
```

toascii

Returns

The *toascii* macro returns the converted character.

See Also

isascii

---

tolower, __tolower ◀

Purpose

Use *_tolower* and *tolower* macros to convert an uppercase ASCII character to lowercase. Use *_tolower* only when you are sure that the character being converted is an uppercase letter.

Syntax

```
#include <ctype.h>
int tolower(int c);
int _tolower(int c);
int c;      Character to be converted
```

Example Call

```
c= tolower('Q'); /* c will become 'q' */
```

Returns

Both macros return the lowercase letter corresponding to *c*.

See Also

toupper, _toupper

---

toupper, __toupper ◀

Purpose

Use the *_toupper* and *toupper* macros to convert a lowercase ASCII character to uppercase. Use *_toupper* only when you are sure that the character being converted is a lowercase letter.

Syntax

```
#include <ctype.h>
int toupper(int c);
int _toupper(int c);
int c;      Character to be converted
```

Example Call

```
c = toupper('q'); /* c will become 'Q' */
```

Returns

Each macro returns the uppercase letter corresponding to *c*.

Example

Example 9-1 reads a line and converts it to uppercase. It calls *toupper* on line 12.

Example 9-1　　This example reads a line and converts it to uppercase.

```
 1:/* Read a line and convert it to uppercase */
 2:#include <stdio.h>
 3:#include <ctype.h>
 4:
 5:main()
 6:{
 7:    char input[81], *p_in;
 8:    puts("Enter a line:");
 9:    gets(input);
10:/* Convert the line to uppercase using 'toupper' */
11:    for(p_in = input; *p_in != '\0'; p_in++)
12:        *p_in = toupper(*p_in);
13:/* Display the result */
14:    printf("\n%s\n", input);
15:}
```

10
String Manipulation

Manipulating strings is a major part of many computer applications. Typically this involves chores such as extracting substrings from the string and comparing or copying one string with another. There is no string data type in C. A string is simply an array of type *char* with a null byte marking the end of the string. Microsoft C has a set of string manipulation routines that provides all the capabilities needed to process strings. These routines are declared in the header file *string.h*.

► strcat, strncat

Purpose

Use the *strcat* function to append the string *string2* to *string1*. Use *strncat* to append only the first *n* characters of *string2* to *string1*.

Syntax

```
#include <string.h>
char *strcat(char *string1, const char *string2);
char *strncat(char *string1, const char *string2, size_t n);
char        *string1;      Destination string
const char *string2;       String to be appended to the first one
size_t       n;            Number of characters of string2 to be appended
                           to string1 by strncat
```

Example Call

```
char metoo[7] = "Me ";
char id[16] = "ID = ";
strcat(metoo, "too");  /* Result is "Me too"      */
strncat(id, name, 10); /* id is first 10 char of name */
```

Returns

Both functions return a pointer to the concatenated string, which is *string1*.

See Also

```
strcpy, strncpy
```

Example

Examples 10-1 and 10-2, respectively, use *strcat* and *strncat* to concatenate strings.

► strchr, strrchr

Purpose

Use the *strchr* function to search for the first occurrence of the character *c* in the null-terminated string *string*. The terminating null character (\0) is included in the search; it can also be the character to be located. The *strrchr* function is similar, except that it locates the last occurrence of the character *c* in *string*.

strchr, strrchr

Syntax

```
#include <string.h>
char *strchr(const char *string, int c);
char *strrchr(const char *string, int c);
const char *string;      String to be searched
int       c;             Character to be located
```

Example Call

```
char line_cost[] = "10 units at $1.20 ea. = $12.00";
total_cost = strrchr(line_cost, '$');
/* total_cost will be "$12.00" */
cost_is = strchr("Estimated cost = $120", '$');
/* cost_is will be "$120"  */
```

Returns

If the character *c* is found, each function returns a pointer to the appropriate occurrence of *c* in *string*. If the search fails, they return NULL.

See Also

```
strcspn, strpbrk, strstr
```

---

strcmp, strcmpi, stricmp, strncmp, ◀ strnicmp

Purpose

Use the *strcmp* function to compare *string1* and *string2* lexigraphically. Use *strncmp* when you want to compare at most the first *n* characters of the strings. The *strcmpi* and *stricmp* functions are similar to *strcmp* except that they ignore the case of the letters during comparison. Similarly, *strnicmp* is a case-insensitive version of *strncmp*.

Syntax

```
#include <string.h>
int strcmp(const char *string1, const char *string2);
int strcmpi(const char *string1, const char *string2);
int stricmp(const char *string1, const char *string2);
int strncmp(const char *string1, const char *string2, size_t
                                                          n);
int strnicmp(const char *string1, const char *string2, size_t
                                                          n);
const char *string1;    First null-terminated string
const char *string2;    Second null-terminated string
size_t    n;            Number of characters of above strings to be
                        compared by strncmp and strnicmp
```

Example Call

```
if( strcmp(username, "dbmgr") != 0 ) exit(1);
if( stricmp(answer, "yes") == 0 ) delete_file(fname);
if(strncmp(command, "quit", 4) == 0) quit_program();
```

Returns

Each function returns an integer greater than, equal to, or less than 0 accordingly as *string1* is greater than, equal to, or less than *string2*.

See Also

memcmp

► strcpy, strncpy

Use *strcpy* to copy *string2* to *string1*. Use *strncpy* to copy only the first *n* characters of *string2* to *string1*. Note that if *n* is less than the length of *string2*, *strncpy* will not append a null character to the copy in *string1*.

Syntax

```
#include <string.h>
char *strcpy(char *string1, const char *string2);
char *strncpy(char *string1, const char *string2, size_t n);
char       *string1;      Destination string
const char *string2;      Null-terminated source string
size_t      n;            Number of characters to be copied by strncpy
```

Example Call

```
strcpy(dos_command, "DIR");
strncpy(fname, "tmp12345678", 8); /* fname = "tmp12345" */
```

Returns

Both functions return the argument *string1*.

See Also

memcpy, memmove, strcat, strncat

► strcspn, strspn

Purpose

Use the *strcspn* function to compute the length of the maximum initial segment of *string1* that consists entirely of characters not in *string2*. The *strspn* function, on the other hand, is used to find the length of the maximum initial segment of *string1* that consists entirely of characters from the string *string2*.

Syntax

```
#include <string.h>
size_t strcspn(const char *string1, const char *string2);
size_t strspn(const char *string1, const char *string2);
const char *string1;     String to be searched
const char *string2;     String describing set of characters
```

Example Call

```
char *input = "280ZX";
first_nondigit_at = strspn(input, "1234567890");
/* first_nondigit_at will be  3 */
first_q = strcspn("soliloquy", "q"); /* first_q = 6 */
```

Returns

Each function returns the length of the segment that meets its criterion.

See Also

strchr, strpbrk, strrchr

---

 strdup ◀

Purpose

Use the *strdup* function to allocate memory and copy *string* to the newly allocated space. You are responsible for freeing the space when it is no longer needed.

Syntax

```
#include <string.h>
char *strdup(const char *string);
const char *string;     Null-terminated string to be duplicated
```

Example Call

```
saved_command = strdup(command);
```

Returns

If the *strdup* function succeeds, it returns a pointer to the new copy of the string. If memory allocation fails, *strdup* returns a NULL.

See Also

free, strcat, strcpy

▶ strerror, __strerror

Purpose

Use the *strerror* function to obtain the system error message corresponding to the error number *errnum*. Use __*strerror* to construct an error message consisting of your message *string* (provided it is not NULL) concatenated with a system message corresponding to the last system error.

Syntax

```
#include <string.h>
char *strerror(int errnum);
char *_strerror(char *string);
int       errnum;       Error number for strerror
char      *string;      String containing user-supplied error message
                        for _strerror
```

Example Call

```
error_message_1 = strerror(errno);
error_message_2 = _strerror("Error opening file");
```

Returns

Both functions return the pointer to the error message. It is up to you to print the message.

See Also

perror

▶ strlen

Purpose

Use *strlen* to find the length of *string* in bytes, not counting the terminating null character.

Syntax

```
#include <string.h>
size_t strlen(const char *string);
const char *string;       Null-terminated string whose length is to be
                          returned
```

Example Call

```
length = strlen("Ivy"); /* length is 3 */
```

Returns

The *strlen* function returns the number of characters in *string* not counting the terminating null character.

See Also

strcspn

---

strlwr, strupr ◄

Purpose

Use *strlwr* and *strupr* to convert all letters in *string* to lowercase and uppercase, respectively.

Syntax

```
#include <string.h>
char *strlwr(char *string);
char *strupr(char *string);
char       *string;     Null-terminated string to be converted
```

Example Call

```
char command[] = "QUIT";
strlwr(command); /* Now command = "quit" */
strupr("help"); /* converts it to "HELP" */
```

Returns

Both functions return *string*.

See Also

tolower, toupper

---

strnset, strset ◄

Purpose

Use *strnset* to set the first *n* characters in *string*, excluding the terminating null (\0), to *c*. The *strset* function sets the entire string to *c*.

Syntax

```
#include <string.h>
```

```
char *strnset(char *string, int c, size_t n);
char *strset(char *string, int c);          •
char    *string;      Null-terminated string
int     c;            Value that will be copied into string
size_t  n;            Number of characters to be set by strnset
```

Example Call

```
char password[16], all_zzz[80];
strset(password, 'x');          /* Set password to all 'x' */
strnset(all_zzz, 'z', 40);      /* First 40 chars to 'z'   */
```

Returns

Both functions return the argument *string*.

See Also

memset

► strpbrk

Purpose

Use the *strpbrk* function to locate the first occurrence in *string1* of any character in *string2*.

Syntax

```
#include <string.h>
char *strpbrk(const char *string1, const char *string2);
const char *string1;      String to be searched
const char *string2;      String describing set of characters to be located
```

Example Call

```
first_vowel = strpbrk(word, "aeiou");
```

Returns

If successful, the *strpbrk* function returns a pointer to the first occurrence of any character from *string2* in *string1*. If the search fails, *strpbrk* returns NULL.

See Also

strchr, strcspn, strrchr, strspn

Example

Example 10-3 uses *strpbrk* to extract the first syllable in a word.

strpbrk

strrev

Purpose

Use *strrev* to reverse the order of characters in a string.

Syntax

```
char *strrev(char *string);
char       *string;      Null-terminated string to be reversed
```

Example Call

```
strrev(input_string);
```

Returns

The *strrev* function returns its argument *string*.

See Also

strcpy, strncpy

strstr ◄

Purpose

Use *strstr* to locate the first occurrence of *string2* as a substring of *string1*.

Syntax

```
#include <string.h>
char *strstr(const char *string1, const char *string2);
const char *string1;    String to be searched
const char *string2;    String to be located
```

Example Call

```
    char input[]="The account number is MCEG-88-10-15";
    acc_no = strstr(input, "MCEG");
/* Now the string acc_no will be "MCEG-88-10-15" */
```

Returns

If successful, the *strstr* function returns a pointer to the first oc-currence of *string2* as a substring in *string1*. If the search fails, *strstr* returns a NULL.

See Also

strchr, strcspn, strpbrk

▶ strtok

Purpose

Use the *strtok* function to retrieve a token or substring from *string1*. The token is marked by delimiting characters given in the second string argument *string2*. All tokens in a particular string *string1* can be extracted through successive calls to *strtok* as follows. Make the first call to *strtok* with the string to be "tokenized" as the first argument. Provide as the second argument a string composed from the delimiting characters. After that, call *strtok* with a NULL as the first argument and the delimiting characters appropriate for that token in the second string. This will tell *strtok* to continue returning tokens from the old *string1*.

Note that the set of delimiters can change in each call to *strtok*. In the process of separating tokens, *strtok* modifies the string *string1*. It inserts null characters in the place of delimiters to convert tokens to C strings.

Syntax

```
#include <string.h>
char *strtok(char *string1, const char *string2);
char       *string1;      String from which tokens are returned
const char *string2;      String describing set of characters that delimit
                          tokens
```

Example Call

```
next_token = strtok(input, "\t, ");
```

Returns

The first call to *strtok* with the argument *string1* will return a pointer to the first token. Subsequent calls with a NULL as the first argument will return the next token. When there are no more tokens left, *strtok* returns a NULL.

See Also

```
strcspn, strpbrk, strspn
```

Example

Example 10-4 shows a simple program that extracts tokens from a string.

Example 10-1   This program prompts you for the first name, last name, and middle initial. Then it uses *strcat* to construct the full name and print a message.

```
1:#include <stdio.h>
```

```
 2:#include <string.h>
 3:main()
 4:{
 5:    char fullname[80], last[40], middle[10];
 6:    printf("Enter your first name: ");
 7:    gets(fullname);
 8:    printf("Last name: ");
 9:    gets(last);
10:    printf("Middle initial: ");
11:    gets(middle);
12:/* Append the parts together to get full name */
13:    strcat(fullname," ");
14:    strcat(fullname, middle);
15:    strcat(fullname," ");
16:    strcat(fullname, last);
17:    printf("Greetings! %s\n", fullname);
18:}
```

Example 10-2   This program uses *strncat* to generate and print the sequence of strings:

```
a
ab
abc
abcd
abcde
...
...
abcdefghijklmnopqrstuvwxyz
```

```
 1:#include <stdio.h>
 2:#include <string.h>
 3:char result[40] = "a";
 4:char rest[] = "bcdefghijklmnopqrstuvwxyz";
 5:unsigned length = sizeof(rest)/sizeof(char);
 6:main()
 7:{
 8:    unsigned i;
 9:    for(i = 0; i<length; i++, result[1]='\0')
10:    {
11:        strncat(result, rest, i);
12:/* Show the current result */
13:        printf("%s\n", result);
14:    }
15:}
```

Example 10-3   This example uses *strpbrk* to locate the first occurrence of a vowel in a word and print the word up to and including the vowel. (This will tend to extract the first syllable from the word.)

```
 1:#include <stdio.h>
 2:#include <string.h>
 3:char *vowels = "aeiou";
```

```
 4:main()
 5:{
 6:    char str1[80], *result;
 7:    printf("Enter a word: ");
 8:    gets(str1);
 9:    if ((result = strpbrk(str1, vowels)) == NULL)
10:    {
11:        printf("No vowels in word\n");
12:    }
13:    else
14:    {
15:        printf("First syllable in %s ", str1);
16:/* Put a null character just after the first vowel */
17:        result++;
18:        *result = '\0';
19:        printf("is: %s\n", str1);
20:    }
21:}
```

Example 10-4   This program reads a string and separates it into tokens. We assume that the tokens are separated by blank spaces, tabs, or commas. This process of converting the input strings to tokens is known as "parsing" and is one of the first things any command interpreter or compiler has to do.

```
 1:#include <stdio.h>
 2:#include <string.h>
 3:char tokensep[] = " \t,";
 4:main()
 5:{
 6:    int i = 0;
 7:    char buf[80], *token;
 8:    printf("Enter a string of tokens separated by comma"
 9:           " or blank:");
10:    gets(buf);
11:/*Call strtok once to get first token and initialize it*/
12:    token = strtok(buf, tokensep);
13:/*Keep calling strtok to get all tokens             */
14:    while(token != NULL)
15:    {
16:        i++;
17:        printf("Token %d = %s\n", i, token);
18:        token = strtok(NULL, tokensep);
19:    }
20:}
```

11
Searching and Sorting

Searching and sorting are commonplace in many applications. All commercial data base programs have these capabilities. If you need search and sort in your programs, Microsoft C makes your job easier by providing four library routines for sorting and searching lists in memory. These routines are declared in the file *stdlib.h*.

▶ bsearch

Purpose

Use the *bsearch* function to search a sorted array that begins at the address *base* and is composed of *num* elements, each of size *width* bytes. The argument *key* points to the value being sought. The argument *compare* is a pointer to a function that you write to compare the elements you are sorting. The function should return a negative, zero, or positive value accordingly as *elem1* is less than, equal to, or greater than *elem2*. Note that you can use the *qsort* routine to sort the array before calling *bsearch*.

Syntax

```
#include <stdlib.h>    or    #include <search.h>
void *bsearch(const void *key, const void *base, size_t num,
              size_t width, int (*compare)(const void *elem1,
              const void *elem2));
```

`const void *key;`	*Pointer to element value to be located*
`const void *base;`	*Pointer to beginning of array being searched*
`size_t    num;`	*Number of elements in array*
`size_t    width;`	*Size of each elements in bytes*
`int  (*compare)(const void *elem1,`	
`     const void *elem2);`	*Pointer to a function that compares two elements* elem1 *and* elem2 *each of type* const void *

Example Call

```
int mycompare(const void *, const void *);
result = (char **) bsearch((const void *)keyword,
                           (const void *)envp,
                           (size_t)count,
                           (size_t)sizeof(char *),
                           mycompare);
```

Returns

If the search is successful, *bsearch* returns a pointer to the first occurrence of the value *key* in the array. If the value is not found, it returns NULL.

See Also

lfind, lsearch, qsort

Example

Line 29 in Example 11-1 calls *bsearch* to search for a keyword in a sorted array.

bsearch

lfind, lsearch ◄

Purpose

The *lfind* and *lsearch* functions are similar to *bsearch*, but they can search unsorted arrays. Additionally, if the search fails, *lsearch* adds to the array the element being sought.

Syntax

```
#include <stdlib.h>
char *lfind(char *key, char *base, unsigned *p_num,
            unsigned width, int (*compare)(void *elem1,
            void *elem2));
char *lsearch(char *key, char *base, unsigned *p_num,
              unsigned width, int (*compare)(void *elem1,
              void *elem2));
```

char	*key;	*Pointer to element value to be located*
char	*base;	*Pointer to beginning of array being searched*
unsigned	*p_num;	*Pointer to location where number array elements are stored*
unsigned	width;	*Size of each elements in bytes*
int	(*compare)(void *elem1,	
	void *elem2);	*Pointer to a function that compares two elements* elem1 *and* elem2 *each of type* void *

Example Call

```
int mycompare(void *, void *);
result = (char **) lsearch((char *)keyword, (char *)envp,
                           &count, sizeof(char *),
                           mycompare);
```

Returns

If the search is successful, each function returns a pointer to the first occurrence of the value *key* in the array. If the value is not found, *lfind* returns NULL, and *lsearch* adds the *key* to the table and returns a pointer to the new element.

See Also

bsearch, qsort

qsort ◄

Purpose

Use the *qsort* function to sort in ascending order an array that begins at the address *base* and is composed of *num* elements, each of size *width* bytes. See *bsearch* for details of *compare*.

Syntax

```
#include <stdlib.h>   or   #include <search.h>
void qsort(void *base, size_t num, size_t width,
           int (*compare)(const void *elem1, const void
                                                 *elem2));
```

void	*base;	*Pointer to beginning of array being sorted*
size_t	num;	*Number of elements in array*
size_t	width;	*Size of each element in bytes*
int (*compare)(const void *elem1, const void *elem2);		*Pointer to a function that compares two elements* elem1 *and* elem2 *each of type* const void *

Example Call

```
int compare(const void *, const void *);
qsort((void *) envp, (size_t)count,
      (size_t)sizeof(char *), compare);
```

See Also

bsearch, lfind, lsearch

Example

Line 19 in Example 11-1 calls *qsort* to sort an array.

Example 11-1   In Microsoft C under MS-DOS, the *main* function is invoked with three arguments, the first two are the familiar number of strings in the command line and the command line itself. The third argument is the MS-DOS environment table, which is also an array of strings. This program accepts a keyword on the command line and uses *bsearch* to search for the string beginning with this keyword in the environment table. It sorts the environment table first using *qsort*, prints it, and then calls *bsearch* to perform the search. Note that the end of the environment table is marked by a NULL entry. Use this information to count the number of entries in the table.

```
1:#include <stdio.h>
2:#include <string.h>
3:#include <stdlib.h>
4:int mycompare(const void *, const void *);
5:main(int argc, char **argv, char **envp)
6:{
7:    unsigned int i, count;
8:    char **p_table, **result;
9:    if(argc < 2)
10:   {
11:    printf("Usage: %s <KEYWORD>\n", argv[0]);
12:    exit(0);
```

qsort

```
13:    }
14:/* Find length of environment table                    */
15:    for(count = 0, p_table = envp;
16:        *p_table != NULL;
17:        p_table++, count++);        /* a null loop    */
18:/* Sort the environment table using "qsort"            */
19:    qsort((void *) envp, (size_t)count,
20:          (size_t)sizeof(char *), mycompare);
21:/* Print sorted environment table                      */
22:    printf("===== Sorted environment table =====\n");
23:    for(i = 0, p_table = envp; i < count; i++)
24:    {
25:     printf("%s\n", *p_table);
26:     p_table++;
27:    }
28:/* Search for the KEY variable in the environment   */
29:    result = (char **) bsearch((const void *)&argv[1],
30:                               (const void *)envp,
31:                               (size_t)count,
32:                               (size_t)sizeof(char *),
33:                               mycompare);
34:    if(result != NULL)
35:    {
36:     printf("\nFound %s in\n%s\n", argv[1], *result);
37:    }
38:    else
39:    {
40:     printf("\n%s not found.\
41:Try with uppercase keyword\n", argv[1]);
42:    }
43:}
44:/*-----------------------------------------------------*/
45:int mycompare(char **arg1, char **arg2)
46:{
47:/* Compare two strings up to the length of the key   */
48:    return(strncmp(*arg1, *arg2, strlen(*arg1)));
49:}
50:
```

Here is a sample output (assuming that you saved the executable program in the file BSEARCH.EXE):

```
C:\MCEG\EX>bsearch PROM
===== Sorted environment table =====
COMSPEC=C:\COMMAND.COM
INCLUDE=c:\include
INIT=c:\src\me\ini
LIB=c:\lib
PATH=C:\;C:\DOS3.1;C:\BIN;C:\BOUND;C:\TURBOC;C:
                        \MASM; C:\ZORTECH\BIN
PROMPT=$p$g
TMP=c:\tmp
Found PROM in
PROMPT=$p$g
```

12

Time and Date Functions

The Microsoft C library includes a set of routines for obtaining and displaying date and time information. These routines are declared in the header file *time.h*. The *time* function is at the heart of these routines. It returns the current time in a *time_t* data type. The time is expressed as the number of seconds elapsed since 00:00 hour Greenwich Mean Time (GMT), 1 January 1970. This is how UNIX stores time. There are library routines that convert this time into a printable string or manipulate it in other ways.

▶ asctime

Purpose

Use the *asctime* function to convert to a character string the value of a time stored in the structure of type *tm* at the address *time*. The structure *tm* is defined in *time.h* as follows:

```
struct tm
{
    int tm_sec;   /* seconds after the minute - [0,60] */
    int tm_min;   /* minutes after the hour - [0,59]   */
    int tm_hour;  /* hours since midnight - [0,23]     */
    int tm_mday;  /* day of the month - [1,31]         */
    int tm_mon;   /* months since January - [0,11]     */
    int tm_year;  /* years since 1900                  */
    int tm_wday;  /* days since Sunday - [0,6]         */
    int tm_yday;  /* days since January 1 - [0,365]    */
    int tm_isdst; /* daylight savings time flag        */
};
```

The string prepared by *asctime* will be 26 characters long, counting the null character (\0) at the end and has the form:

```
Thu Oct 20 19:02:39 1988\n\0
```

As the example shows, a 24-hour clock is used for the time.

Syntax

```
#include <time.h>
char *asctime(const struct tm *time);
const struct tm *time;    Pointer to a structure containing time to be
                          converted to a string
```

Example Call

```
printf("The time is %s\n", asctime(&timedata));
```

Returns

The *asctime* function returns a pointer to the static data area where the string is stored.

See Also

ctime, gmtime, localtime, mktime, time

▶ clock

Purpose

Use *clock* to obtain the amount of processor time used by the current process in "number of ticks." The constant CLK _TCK

clock

(defined in *time.h* to be 1000) is the number of ticks per second, so the value returned by *clock* should be divided by CLK_TCK to get the elapsed processor time in seconds.

Syntax

```
#include <time.h>
clock_t clock(void);
```

Example Call

```
ticks_now = clock();
```

Returns

If processor time is available to *clock*, it returns the current time in ticks, cast as a value of type *clock_t*, which is defined in *time.h*. Otherwise, it returns the value -1, cast as *clock_t*.

See Also

```
difftime, time
```

---

ctime ◀

Purpose

Use the *ctime* function to convert to a character string the value of time stored in the variable of type *time_t* at the address *timer*. Calling *ctime* is equivalent to the call *asctime(localtime (timer))*.

Syntax

```
#include <time.h>
char *ctime(const time_t *timer);
const time_t *timer;          Pointer to calendar time
```

Example Call

```
printf("Current time = %s\n", ctime(&bintime));
```

Returns

The *ctime* function returns the pointer to the string.

See Also

```
asctime, time
```

Example

Line 11 in Example 12-1 uses *ctime* to convert an encoded *time_t* value to a string.

► difftime

Purpose

Use the *difftime* function to compute the difference between two time values *time2* and *time1*, both of type *time_t*.

Syntax

```
#include <time.h>
double difftime(time_t time2, time_t time1);
time_t time2;      Value of time from which time1 will be subtracted
time_t time1;      Value of time to be subtracted from time2
```

Example Call

```
seconds_used = difftime(oldtime, newtime);
```

Returns

The *difftime* function returns the elapsed time, *time2-time1*, in seconds as a double precision number.

See Also

```
clock, time
```

► ftime

Purpose

Use *ftime* to get the current time and store it in a *timeb* structure, which is defined in the include file *sys\timeb.h* as:

```
struct timeb
{
    time_t          time;     /* Time in UNIX format */
    unsigned short millitm;  /* Milliseconds        */
    short           timezone; /* Difference in minutes
                                 moving westward, between
                                 GMT and local time */
    short           dstflag;  /* Nonzero if daylight
                                 saving is in effect */
};
```

Syntax

```
#include <sys\timeb.h>
void ftime(struct timeb *timeptr);
struct timeb *timeptr;        Pointer to structure of type timeb where time
                              is returned
```

ftime

Example Call

```
ftime(&time_buffer);
```

See Also

```
time, tzset
```

---

gmtime, localtime ◄

Purpose

Use the *gmtime* function to break down a time value of type *time_t* stored at the location *time* into year, month, day, hour, minutes, seconds, and several other fields that it saves in a structure of type *tm* maintained internally. The structure *tm* is defined in *time.h* and shown under *asctime*. The fields set up by *gmtime* will be in GMT. The *localtime* function works similarly except that it sets up the fields for the local time.

Syntax

```
#include <time.h>
struct tm *gmtime(const time_t *time);
struct tm *localtime(const time_t *time);
const time_t *time;        Pointer to calendar time
```

Example Call

```
t_gmt = gmtime(&bintime);
t_local = localtime(&bintime);
```

Returns

Each function returns a pointer to the *tm* structure where the converted time is stored. If GMT is not available, *gmtime* returns a NULL.

See Also

```
asctime, mktime, time, tzset
```

Line 14 in Example 12-2 uses *localtime* to convert a *time_t* value into a broken-down time.

---

mktime ◄

Purpose

Use the *mktime* function to convert the local time currently in the structure of type *tm* at the address *timeptr* to a value of type

mktime

time_t. Essentially, the local time given in the form of year, month, day, and so on, is converted to the number of seconds elapsed since 00:00:00 hours GMT, January 1, 1970. This is the same format in which *time* returns the current time and is the format used in the argument to the functions *ctime*, *difftime*, and *localtime*.

Two fields in the structure of type *tm* are ignored by *mktime*. These are the fields *tm_wday* and *tm_yday*, denoting, respectively, the day of the week and the day of the year. The *mktime* function will set the fields in the *tm* structure to appropriate values before returning.

Syntax

```
#include <time.h>
time_t mktime(struct tm *timeptr);
struct tm *timeptr;        Pointer to structure of type tm where local time is
                           stored
```

Example Call

```
bintime = mktime(&timebuf);
```

Returns

If successful, *mktime* will return the current contents of *timeptr* encoded as a value of type *time_t*. If the local time in *timeptr* cannot be handled by *mktime*, the return value will be a −1 cast to the type *time_t*.

See Also

```
asctime, time
```

Example

Example 12-2 uses *mktime* to implement a utility that prints the date any number of days from the current day.

▶ __strdate, __strtime

Purpose

Use *__strdate* to obtain the current date as a null-terminated eight-character string of the form *10/20/88*. Use *__strtime* to obtain the current time as a null-terminated eight-character string of the form *17:09:35*.

Syntax

```
#include <time.h>
```

__strdate, __strtime

```
char *_strdate(char *date);
char *_strtime(char *time);
char *date;      Pointer to buffer where the current date in the form
                 MM/DD/YY, returned by _strdate
char *time;      Pointer to buffer where the current time in the form
                 HH:MM:SS, returned by _strtime
```

Example Call

```
_strdate(date_buffer);
```

Returns

Both functions return their argument.

See Also

asctime, time

---

time ◀

Purpose

Use the *time* function to get the current date and time (calendar time) encoded as an implementation-dependent value of type *time_t*. If the pointer *timeptr* is not NULL, the encoded time is copied to the location whose address is in *timeptr*.

Syntax

```
#include <time.h>
time_t time(time_t *timeptr);
time_t *timeptr;     Pointer to variable where result will be returned
```

Example Call

```
time(&bintime);
```

Returns

The *time* function returns the calendar time as the number of seconds elapsed since 00:00:00 hour, January 1, 1970.

See Also

ctime, ftime, gmtime, localtime

Example

Line 7 in Example 12-1 and line 13 in Example 12-2 call *time* to get the current calendar time in encoded form.

► tzset

Purpose

Use *tzset* to assign values to the global variables *timezone, daylight*, and *tzname* based on the time zone specified in the environment variable TZ. See *The Waite Group's Microsoft C Bible* for more details.

Syntax

```
#include <time.h>
void tzset(void);
```

Example Call

```
tzset();
```

See Also

ftime, gmtime

► utime

Purpose

Use *utime* to change the "last modified" time stamp of a file to which you have write access. The new time is specified in a *utimbuf* buffer, which is defined in *sys\utime.h* as:

```
struct utimbuf
{
    time_t actime;      /* access time       */
    time_t modtime;     /* modification time */
};
```

Syntax

```
#include <sys\utime.h>
int utime(char *path, struct utimbuf *timeptr);
char          *path;        Path name of file whose last-modified time
                            is set
struct utimbuf *timeptr;    Pointer to a structure through which the
                            modification time is specified (or NULL for
                            current time)
```

Example Call

```
/* Set modification time of file to current time */
    utime(file_name, NULL);
```

utime

Returns

If *utime* is successful, it returns 0. In case of any error, it returns −1 and sets *errno* to an error code.

See Also

time

Example 12-1   This program prints the current date and time.

```
1:#include <stdio.h>
2:#include <time.h>
3:main()
4:{
5:    time_t tnow;
6:/* Get the time in in encoded form */
7:    time(&tnow);
8:/* Convert the time to a string and print it. This
9: * will be your local time.
10: */
11:    printf("Current time = %s\n", ctime(&tnow));
12:}
```

Here is a sample output:

```
Current time = Tue Oct 11 22:08:34 1988
```

Example 12-2   The *mktime* function does not care if the fields in the *tm* data structure are within the valid range or not. In other words, you can set the number of days since first of the month to 45, and *mktime* will adjust other fields (such as making it the next month) to bring all entries to valid ranges. In this example, we use this feature to set up a utility program that prints the date a specified number of days from today. The program accepts as a command-line argument the number of days to look ahead.

```
1:#include <stdio.h>
2:#include <time.h>
3:main(int argc, char **argv)
4:{
5:    time_t    tresult, tnow;
6:    struct tm *tmnow;
7:    if(argc<2)
8:    {
9:        printf("Usage: %s <number of days>\n", argv[0]);
10:        exit(0);
11:    }
12:/* Get todays's date and convert it to a "tm" structure */
13:    time(&tnow);
14:    tmnow = localtime(&tnow);
```

utime

```
15:/* Adjust the number of days */
16:    tmnow->tm_mday += atoi(argv[1]);
17:/* Now call "mktime" to set everything in tmnow */
18:    if((tresult = mktime(tmnow)) == (time_t)-1)
19:    {
20:        printf("mktime failed\n");
21:    }
22:    else
23:    {
24:        printf("%d days from now it'll be %s\n",
25:                atoi(argv[1]), ctime(&tresult));
26:    }
27:}
```

When run with 4 as the argument on *Tue Oct 11 22:11:02 1988*, the program produces the output:

```
4 days from now it'll be Sat Oct 15 22:11:02 1988
```

IV

Microsoft C I/O and System Calls

13

File Manipulation

The file system is a key system component of the PC. All applications and data reside in files. If you develop an application, it is likely to use files for storage of its data and results so that they can be reused at a later date. We cover reading from and writing to files in Chapter 15. This chapter covers the Microsoft C routines that enable us to determine status of a file and to perform certain house-keeping chores to keep the files in order.

► access

Purpose

Use *access* to check if a file exists and if read and/or write operations are permitted on the file. Use one of the values in Table 13-1 for the argument *mode*.

Table 13-1. *mode* Values

Value of *mode*	Interpretation of the Value
00	Check if file exists
02	Check if file has write permission
04	Check if file has read permission
06	Check if file has read and write permission

Syntax

```
#include <io.h>
int access(char *path, int mode);
char *path;     Path name of file being checked
int  mode;      Integer denoting permission setting being checked
```

Example Call

```
if(access("temp.dat", 4) == 0) puts("Data file exists");
```

Returns

If *access* finds that the file or directory specified by *path* exists and allows the access specified by *mode*, it returns 0. Otherwise, it returns −1 and sets *errno* to an error code.

See Also

chmod, fstat, stat

► chmod

Purpose

Use *chmod* to alter the read/write permission settings of a file. The permission settings are specified in terms of constants defined in the include file *sys\stat.h* shown in Table 13-2.

Syntax

```
#include <io.h>
#include <sys\types.h>
```

chmod

```
#include <sys\stat.h>
int chmod(char *path, int pmode);
char *path;      Path name of file whose permission is being changed
int  pmode;      Integer denoting new permission setting for the file
```

Table 13-2. Permission Settings

Constant	Interpretation of the Constant
S_IWRITE	Both reading and writing permitted
S_IREAD	Only reading permitted
S_IREAD | S_IWRITE	Both reading and writing permitted

Example Call

```
chmod("inventory.lis", S_IWRITE);
```

Returns

If *chmod* is successful, it returns 0. Otherwise, it returns −1 and sets *errno* to an error code.

See Also

```
access, fstat, stat
```

Example

Example 13-1 uses *chmod* in a utility that lets you alter the read/write permissions of a file.

---

 chsize ◄

Purpose

Use *chsize* to extend or truncate a file open for unbuffered, unformatted write operations.

Syntax

```
#include <io.h>
int chsize(int handle, long size);
int handle;      Handle of file whose size is being changed
long size;       New length of file in bytes
```

Example Call

```
chsize(filehandle, 0L);  /* Truncate file to zero length */
```

Returns

The *chsize* function returns a 0 to indicate success. In case of error, the return value will be −1, and an error code will be placed in *errno*.

See Also

access, chmod, fstat, stat

▶ filelength

Purpose

Use the *filelength* function to determine the length of a file in bytes.

Syntax

```
#include <io.h>
long filelength(int file_handle);
int file_handle;        Handle of file whose length will be returned
```

Example Call

```
filesize = filelength(filehandle);
```

Returns

The long integer value returned by *filelength* is the size of the file in number of bytes. If an error occurs, the return value is −1L, and *errno* is set to an error code.

See Also

fileno, fstat, stat

▶ fstat, stat

Purpose

Use the *fstat* function to retrieve information about a file specified by *handle*. The *stat* function, on the other hand, returns information about an existing file specified by its path name. The information is in a *stat* structure, which is declared in *sys\stat.h* as:

```
struct stat
{
    dev_t         st_dev;   /* Drive number of disk or handle
                               of device containing the file
                                                             */
    ino_t         st_ino;   /* Unused in MS-DOS. The "i-node"
                               number of file in Unix
                                                             */
    unsigned short st_mode;  /* Bit mask of file's mode
                                                             */
```

```
short         st_nlink; /* Always set to 1 under MS-DOS
                                                          */
short         st_uid;   /* Unused in MS-DOS. For
                            "user-id" under Unix
                                                          */
short         st_gid;   /* Unused in MS-DOS. For
                            "group-id" under Unix
                                                          */
dev_t         st_rdev;  /* Same as the field st_dev
                                                          */
off_t         st_size;  /* Size of file in bytes
                                                          */
time_t        st_atime; /* Time of last modification
                                                          */
time_t        st_mtime; /* Same as st_atime
                                                          */
time_t        st_ctime; /* Same as st_atime
                                                          */
};
```

Syntax

```
#include <sys\types.h>
#include <sys\stat.h>
int fstat(int handle, struct stat *buffer);
int stat(char *path, struct stat *buffer);
int           handle;        Handle of file whose "vital statistics" will be
                             returned by fstat
char          *path;         Path name of file whose "vital statistics" will be
                             returned by stat
struct stat *buffer;         Pointer to structure where the information will
                             be returned
```

Example Call

```
fstat(filehandle, &stat_buffer);
```

Returns

If successful, the functions return 0. Otherwise, they return −1 and set *errno* to an appropriate error code.

See Also

```
access, chmod
```

---

isatty ◄

Purpose

Use the *isatty* function to determine whether a particular file handle refers to a "character device" which, under MS-DOS, means the console, printer, or the serial port.

Syntax

```
#include <io.h>
int isatty(int handle);
int        handle;        Handle you want to check
```

Example Call

```
if(isatty(fileno(stdout)) != 0) puts("stdout is console");
```

Returns

The *isatty* function returns a nonzero value if *handle* refers to a character device. Otherwise, it returns 0.

► locking

Purpose

Use *locking* under MS-DOS Version 3.0 and later, to lock or unlock a number of bytes in a file. This feature is useful when file sharing is enabled by executing the DOS command SHARE. Table 13-3 lists the constants denoting the file-locking modes. These constants are defined in the include file *sys\locking.h*.

Table 13-3. Constants Denoting File-Locking Modes

Locking Mode Name	Interpretation of Locking Mode
LK_LOCK	Locks the specified bytes. If they cannot be locked, *locking* retries every second, up to a maximum of 10 attempts. It returns error if it fails even after these attempts.
LK_RLCK	Same functionality as LK_LOCK.
LK_NBLCK	Locks the specified bytes and returns an error immediately if it fails.
LK_NBRLCK	Same meaning as LK_NBLCK.
LK_UNLCK	Unlock previously locked bytes.

Syntax

```
#include <io.h>
#include <sys\locking.h>
int locking(int handle, int mode, long nbytes);
int    handle;     Handle of file where data is being locked or unlocked
int    mode;       Integer denoting file-locking mode (See Table 13-3.)
long   nbytes;     Number of bytes to be locked or unlocked
```

Example Call

```
locking(handle, LK_NBLCK, 256); /* Lock 256 bytes */
```

locking

Returns

If successful, *locking* returns a 0. Otherwise, it returns −1.

See Also

sopen

__makepath, __splitpath ◄

Purpose

Use _*makepath* to create a full path name composed of a drive letter, directory path, file name, and file extension. The _*splitpath* function performs the reverse task by breaking down a path name into its components.

Syntax

```
#include <dir.h>
void _makepath(char *path, char *drive, char *dir,
               char *fname, char *ext);
void _splitpath(char *path, char *drive, char *dir,
                char *fname, char *ext);
```

char *path;	*Pointer to buffer to hold full path name*
const char *drive;	*Buffer for drive letter*
const char *dir;	*Buffer for directory path*
const char *fname;	*Buffer for file name*
const char *ext;	*Buffer for file extension*

Example Call

```
_makepath(pathname, "c:", "temp", "result", ".dat");
/* path name will be c:\temp\result.dat  */
```

mktemp ◄

Purpose

Use the *mktemp* function to generate unique file names by modifying a given template for the names.

Syntax

```
#include <dir.h>
char *mktemp(char *template);
```

char *template;	*Pattern string to be used in constructing file names*

Example Call

```
char tfilename = "nabaXXXXXX";
mktemp(tfilename);
```

Returns

If successful, *mktemp* returns a pointer to the modified template. In case of any error, it returns NULL.

See Also

tmpfile, tmpnam

► remove, unlink

Purpose

Use *remove* and *unlink* to delete a file specified by its path name.

Syntax

```
#include <stdio.h>
int remove(const char *path);
int unlink(const char *path);
const char *path;       Path name of file to be deleted
```

Example Call

```
remove("c:\\tmp\\tmp01234"); /* Delete temporary file */
```

Returns

If the file is successfully deleted, the functions return 0. Otherwise, they return −1 and set *errno* to an error code.

See Also

system

► rename

Purpose

Use *rename* to change the name of a file or directory specified by its path name.

Syntax

```
#include <stdio.h>
int rename(const char *oldname, const char *newname);
const char *oldname;      Current path name of file or directory
const char *newname;      New path name
```

Example Call

```
/* Copy "text.exe" from c:\tmp to c:\bin and
   give it a new name */
rename("c:\\tmp\\test.exe", "c:\\bin\\grview.exe");
```

Returns

If *rename* is successful, it returns 0. Otherwise, it returns −1 and sets *errno* to an appropriate error code.

See Also

```
creat, fopen, open
```

setmode ◄

Purpose

Use the *setmode* function to set the translation mode of a file identified by *handle*. The translation mode can be either O_BINARY or O_TEXT, which are constants defined in *fcntl.h*.

Syntax

```
#include <io.h>
#include <fcntl.h>
int setmode(int handle, int mode);
int  handle;      Handle of open file
int  mode;        Integer denoting new translation mode
```

Example Call

```
setmode(filehandle, O_BINARY); /* Set file mode to binary */
```

Returns

If successful, *setmode* returns the previous value of the translation mode. Otherwise, it returns −1 and sets *errno* to an error code.

See Also

```
fopen, open
```

umask ◄

Purpose

Use the *umask* function to set the read/write permission mask that will be used to modify the read/write permission settings of all subsequent new files created by this program. The prohibited operation is indicated by one of the constants shown in Table 13-2.

Syntax

```
#include <io.h>
#include <sys\types.h>
#include <sys\stat.h>
int umask(int pmode);
int  pmode;        Permission mask to be used in all subsequent new files
```

Example Call

```
/* Make all future files read-only */
oldmask = umask(S_IWRITE);
```

Returns

The *umask* function returns the previous value of the permission mask.

See Also

```
creat, open, sopen
```

Example 13-1   This is a small utility program using *chmod* that allows the user to change the read/write permission of a file. Assume that the command-line syntax is: "CHMOD ⟨pathname⟩ ⟨permission⟩" where "permission" is a single character R or W to indicate read-only and both read-write (assuming that the executable program is named CHMOD.EXE).

```
 1:#include <stdio.h>
 2:#include <sys\types.h>
 3:#include <sys\stat.h>
 4:#include <io.h>
 5:main(int argc, char **argv)
 6:{
 7:     int pmode=-999;
 8:     if(argc < 3)
 9:     {
10:         printf(
11:            "Usage: %s <pathname> <R|W>\n", argv[0]);
12:     }
13:     else
14:     {
15:/* Convert last argument to permission code          */
16:         if(argv[2][0]=='R') pmode = S_IREAD;
17:         if(argv[2][0]=='W') pmode = S_IREAD|S_IWRITE;
18:         if(pmode==-999)
19:         {
20:             printf("Unknown permission: %s\n",
21:                     argv[2]);
```

umask

```
22:          exit(1);
23:      }
24:      if(chmod(argv[1], pmode) == -1)
25:      {
26:          perror("Error in \"chmod\"");
27:      }
28:   }
29:}
```

14

Directory Manipulation

MS-DOS, like UNIX, uses a hierarchical file system allowing you to organize your files under directories and subdirectories. The directory manipulation routines in Microsoft C provide the basic tools necessary to create, modify, and remove directories from your C program.

▶ chdir, mkdir, rmdir

Purpose

Use *chdir* to change the current working directory, *mkdir* to create a new directory, and *rmdir* to remove an empty directory.

Syntax

```
#include <direct.h>
int chdir(char *path);
int mkdir(char *path);
int rmdir(char *path);
char *path;      Path name of directory
```

Example Call

```
chdir("c:\\bin\\sample");
mkdir("c:\\waite\\tceg"); /* c:\waite must already exist */
rmdir("c:\\temp\\last");  /* c:\temp\last must be empty  */
```

Returns

When successful, each function returns 0. In case of error, they return −1 and set *errno* to an error code.

See Also

_dos_setdrive, getcwd

▶ getcwd

Purpose

Use *getcwd* to get the full path name of the current working directory, including the drive name.

Syntax

```
#include <direct.h>
char *getcwd(char *path, int numchars);
char *path;       Buffer where path name of current working directory is
                  returned
int  numchars;    Number of bytes available in the buffer for path name
```

Example Call

```
getcwd(path_buffer, 80);
```

getcwd

Returns

The *getcwd* function returns a pointer to the buffer where the path name is stored. If *path* is NULL, the return value is a pointer to the buffer allocated to hold the path name. In case of error, it returns NULL.

See Also

chdir, _dos_getdrive

__searchenv ◄

Purpose

Use *__searchenv* to search for a particular file in a list of directories including the current working directory and those defined in the environment variable *env_var*.

Syntax

```
#include <stdlib.h>
void _searchenv(char *filename, char *env_var, char *path);
char *filename;      Name of file to find
char *env_var;       Environment variable that defines list of directories to
                     search through
char *path;          Buffer you supply to hold the full path name of file if
                     it is found
```

Example Call

```
_searchenv("CL.EXE", "PATH", buffer);
```

See Also

chdir, _dos_findfirst, _dos_findnext, getenv, _makepath, _splitpath

Example

Example 14-1 uses *__searchenv* in a utility that locates files.

Example 14-1   Write a program that will accept a file name and search for that file in all the directories listed in the PATH environment variable. If found, print the full path name of the file. Use *__searchenv* to locate the file.

```
1:#include <stdio.h>
2:#include <stdlib.h>
3:main(int argc, char **argv)
4:{
5:    char path_buffer[80];
6:    printf("This program searches for a file in all\n"
```

```
 7:                "the directories specified in the PATH \n"
 8:                "environment variable\n");
 9:     if(argc < 2)
10:     {
11:         printf("Usage: %s <filename>\n", argv[0]);
12:         exit(0);
13:     }
14:/* Use "_searchenv" to locate the file */
15:     _searchenv(argv[1], "PATH", path_buffer);
16:     if(path_buffer[0] == '\0')
17:     {
18:         printf("File: %s not found\n", argv[1]);
19:     }
20:     else
21:     {
22:         printf("Found as: %s\n", path_buffer);
23:     }
24:}
25:
```

15
Input and Output Routines

The C programming language has no built-in capability to perform any input and output (I/O). This task is the responsibility of the library accompanying the C compiler. Fortunately, the C library under UNIX has a core set of routines that constitute the de facto standard I/O library (until, at least, the ANSI standard for C is finalized). The Microsoft C library includes this UNIX core set together with a group of I/O routines that provide access to various hardware in the PC. Microsoft C also adheres to the I/O library specifications of the proposed ANSI standard for C, which is likely to be formally adopted in the near future.

The Microsoft C library has three types of I/O routines: the stream routines, followed by the low-level file I/O routines, and finally the console and port I/O routines.

The "stream" routines refer to I/O performed using the model of files as a stream of bytes together with a buffer associated with a file. The "buffer" is a temporary storage area for the stream of bytes being read from or written to the file. The "low-level" routines are similar except that they do not use a buffer. The "console and port I/O" is meant for direct input and output from the keyboard, the monitor, and any peripheral devices (e.g., the serial adapter) attached to the PC.

Note that the reference entries for the I/O routines are organized into three categories: stream I/O, low-level I/O, and console and port I/O.

► clearerr

Purpose

Use the *clearerr* function to reset the error and end-of-file indicator of the file *stream*.

Syntax

```
#include <stdio.h>
void clearerr(FILE *stream);
FILE *stream;        Stream whose error flag is cleared
```

Example Call

```
clearerr(outfile);
```

See Also

feof, ferror

Example

Line 44 in Example 15-1 uses *clearerr* to reset the error flag after an error occurs during file I/O.

► fclose, fcloseall

Purpose

Use *fclose* to close *stream*. The *fcloseall* function closes all open files except the preopened streams *stdin*, *stdout*, *stderr*, *stdaux*, and *stdprn*.

Syntax

```
#include <stdio.h>
int fclose(FILE *stream);
int fcloseall(void);
FILE *stream;        Pointer to file to be closed
```

Example Call

```
fclose(infile);
number_closed = fcloseall();
```

Returns

If the file is successfully closed, *fclose* returns 0, and *fcloseall* returns the number of files it closed. In case of an error, both functions return EOF.

fclose, fcloseall

See Also

fopen, freopen

Example

Lines 57 and 58 in Example 15-1 call *fclose* to close files before exiting the program.

Stream I/O **fdopen ◄**

Purpose

Use *fdopen* to associate a buffer with a file that has been opened for unbuffered, unformatted I/O. This will allow subsequent buffered, formatted read/write operations on the file. See *fopen* for a description of the *access_mode* strings.

Syntax

```
#include <stdio.h>
FILE *fdopen(int handle, char *access_mode);
int handle;                Handle of open file being upgraded for buffered
                           I/O
char *access_mode;         A character string denoting whether file is being
                           opened for read, write (See Table 15-1.)
```

Example Call

datafile = fdopen(handle, "rb");

Returns

If successful, *fdopen* returns a pointer to the stream associated with the file. In case of an error, *fdopen* returns a NULL.

Stream I/O **feof, ferror ◄**

Purpose

Use the *feof* and *ferror* macros, respectively, to determine whether the end of a file was reached, or an error occurred during a file I/O.

Syntax

```
#include <stdio.h>
int feof(FILE *stream);
int ferror(FILE *stream);
FILE *stream;      Stream whose status is being checked
```

Example Call

```
if (feof(infile) != 0) printf("File ended\n");
if (ferror(infile) != 0) printf("Error detected\n");
```

Returns

If the condition being checked is true, the macros return a non-zero value. Otherwise, they return 0.

See Also

```
clearerr, fclose, rewind
```

Example

Lines 40 and 42 of Example 15-1 use *ferror* and *feof* to check for error and end-of-file, respectively.

► fflush, flushall   *Stream I/O*

Purpose

Use the *fflush* function to process ("flush") the current contents of the buffer associated with *stream*. The *flushall* function, on the other hand, flushes all buffers associated with all open streams.

Syntax

```
#include <stdio.h>
int fflush(FILE *stream);
int flushall(void);
FILE *stream;        Stream whose buffer is being flushed
```

Example Call

```
fflush(stdin);
```

Returns

If the buffer is successfully flushed, *fflush* returns a 0, and *flushall* returns the total number of buffers it has flushed. In case of an error, *fflush* returns EOF.

See Also

```
fclose, fopen
```

fflush, flushall

Stream I/O   **fgetc, fgetchar ◄**

Purpose

Use *fgetc* and *fgetchar* to read a single character from *stream* and
from *stdin*, respectively.

Syntax

```
#include <stdio.h>
int fgetc(FILE *stream);
int fgetchar(void);
FILE        *stream;       Stream from which a character is read by fgetc
```

Example Call

```
char_read = fgetc(infile);
c = fgetchar();
```

Returns

If there are no errors, both functions return the character read.
Otherwise, they return EOF. You should call *ferror* and *feof* to
determine if there really was an error or the file simply reached
its end.

See Also

fputc, fputchar, getc, putc, putchar

Stream I/O   **fgetpos ◄**

Purpose

Use *fgetpos* to get and save the current position where reading or
writing will take place in *stream*. Use *fsetpos* to set the position
in *stream*.

Syntax

```
#include <stdio.h>
int fgetpos(FILE *stream, fpos_t *current_pos);
int fsetpos(FILE *stream, const fpos_t *new_pos);
FILE            *stream;        Stream whose position is retrieved
                                or set
fpos_t          *current_pos;   Pointer to location where file's
                                current position is returned by
                                fgetpos
const fpos_t    *new_pos;       Pointer to location containing new
                                value of file position for use by
                                fsetpos
```

Example Call

```
fgetpos(infile, &saved_pos);
fsetpos(infile, &new_pos);
```

Returns

Both functions return zero when successful. In case of error, they return a nonzero value and set *errno* to an error code.

See Also

```
fseek, ftell
```

► fgets   *Stream I/O*

Purpose

Use the *fgets* function to read a line from *stream*. The line is read until a newline (\n) character is encountered or until the number of characters read reaches *maxchar−1*.

Syntax

```
#include <stdio.h>
char *fgets(char *string, int maxchar, FILE *stream);
char *string;      Pointer to buffer where characters will be stored
int maxchar;       Maximum number of characters that can be stored
FILE *stream;      Stream from which to read
```

Example Call

```
fgets(buffer, 80, infile);
```

Returns

If there are no errors, *fgets* returns the argument *string*. Otherwise, it returns a NULL.

See Also

```
fputs, gets, puts
```

Example

Line 38 in Example 15-1 calls *fgets* to read a line from a file.

► fileno   *Stream I/O*

Purpose

Use the *fileno* macro, defined in *stdio.h*, to obtain the handle of

fileno

the file currently associated with *stream*. You need the file handle to use some file I/O routines in the Microsoft C library.

Syntax

```
#include <stdio.h>
int fileno(FILE *stream);
FILE *stream;      Stream whose handle is to be returned
```

Example Call

```
handle = fileno(stream);
```

Returns

The integer value returned by *fileno* is the handle of the specified file. The return value is undefined if the argument *stream* does not correspond to an open file.

See Also

fopen

Stream I/O **fopen ◄**

Purpose

Use *fopen* to open the file whose name is in the string *filename* and associate a stream with it. The argument *access_mode* contains one of the strings from Table 15-1.

Table 15-1. Access Modes When Opening Files for Stream I/O

Access Mode String	Interpretation of the Access Mode
"r"	File will be opened for read operations only. The *fdopen* function will fail if the file already does not exist.
"w"	Open a new file for writing. If the file already exists, its contents will be destroyed.
"a"	Open file for appending. A new file is created if the named file does not exist.
"r+"	Open an existing file for both read and write operations. Error if file does not exist.
"w+"	Create a file and open it for both reading and writing. If file already exists, all current contents are destroyed.
"a+"	Open file for reading and appending. Create a new file if one does not exist.

In addition to the basic access modes shown in Table 15-1, one of the characters from Table 15-2 can be appended to each of the strings in Table 15-1 to specify how the contents of the file are to be translated. Note that the character denoting the translation mode can come before or after the + in the strings above. For example, "w+b" is considered to be the same as "wb+" and means create the file and open it for reading and writing in binary mode.

Table 15-2. File Translation Modes for Stream I/O

Translation Mode	Interpretation of the Translation Mode
b	File is opened in untranslated or binary mode. Every character in the file is read as is without the changes described below.
t	File is opened in translated mode. This is a Microsoft C extension and not an ANSI standard mode. Its purpose is to accommodate MS-DOS file conventions. In this mode the following interpretations will be in effect: 1. Carriage Return-Line Feed (CR-LF) combinations on input are translated to single line feeds. During output, single line feed characters are translated to CR-LF pairs. 2. During input, the Ctrl-Z character is interpreted as the end-of-file character.

If no translation mode is specified, the default mode is determined by the global variable _fmode, which is declared in the header file *stdio.h*.

Syntax

```
#include <stdio.h>
FILE *fopen(const char *filename, const char *access_mode);
const char *filename;        Path name of file to be opened
const char *access_mode;     A character string denoting whether file is
                             being opened for read, write (See Table
                             15-1.)
```

Example Call

```
input_file = fopen("data.in", "rb");
```

Returns

If the file is successfully opened, *fopen* returns a pointer to the stream. In case of an error, it returns a NULL.

See Also

```
fclose, fcloseall, fdopen, freopen, open
```

Example

Examples 15-1 and 15-2 use *fopen* to open files for I/O.

fopen

Stream I/O   **fprintf** ◄

Purpose

Use the *fprintf* function to format and write character strings
and values of C variables to *stream*. See *printf* for a description
of the argument *format_string*.

Syntax

```
#include <stdio.h>
int fprintf(FILE *stream, const char *format_string,...);
FILE *stream;                    Stream to which the output goes
const char *format_string;       Format to be used for output
...                              Variables being printed
```

Example Call

```
fprintf(resultfile, "The result is %f\n", result);
```

Returns

The *fprintf* function returns the number of characters it has
printed.

See Also

```
printf, sprintf, vfprintf, vprintf, vsprintf
```

Stream I/O   **fputc, fputchar** ◄

Purpose

Use *fputc* and *fputchar* to write the character *c* to *stream* and to
stdout, respectively.

Syntax

```
#include <stdio.h>
int fputc(int c, FILE *stream);
int fputchar(int c);
int c;           Character to be written
FILE *stream;    Stream to which fputc writes the character
```

Example Call

```
fputc('X', p_datafile);
fputchar('q');
```

Returns

If there are no errors, both functions return the character written. Otherwise, they return EOF.

fputc, fputchar

See Also

```
fgetc, fgetchar, getc, getchar, putc, putchar
```

► fputs, puts   *Stream I/O*

Purpose

Use the *fputs* function to write *string* to *stream*. The *puts* function is similar, except that it writes to *stdout* and sends a newline character (\n) after the string.

Syntax

```
#include <stdio.h>
int fputs(char *string, FILE *stream);
int puts(const char *string);
const char *string;      Null-terminated character string to be output
FILE        *stream;     Stream to which fputs writes
```

Example Call

```
fputs("Sample Input Data", p_datafile);
puts("Do you really want to quit? ");
```

Returns

In Microsoft C 5.0 and 5.1, both functions return 0 if successful. In earlier versions, when all is well, they return the last character printed. In case of error, they return EOF.

See Also

```
fgets, gets
```

Example

Line 52 in Example 15-1 uses *fputs* to write a string to a file.

► fread, fwrite   *Stream I/O*

Purpose

Use the *fread* function to read *count* data items, each *size* bytes long, from the current position in *stream* into *inbuf*. Similarly, the *fwrite* function writes data from *outbuf* to *stream*. The current file position is updated after the I/O.

Syntax

```
#include <stdio.h>
```

fread, fwrite

```
size_t fread(void *inbuf, size_t size, size_t count,
                                FILE *stream);
size_t fwrite(const void *outbuf, size_t size, size_t count,
                                FILE *stream);
```

void	*inbuf;	*Pointer to memory where* fread *will store the bytes it reads*
const void	*outbuf;	*Pointer to buffer in memory from where* fwrite *will get the bytes it writes*
size_t	size;	*Size in bytes of each data item*
size_t	count;	*Maximum number of items to be transferred*
FILE	*stream;	*Stream with which I/O is performed*

Example Call

```
numread = fread(buffer, sizeof(char), 80, infile);
numwrite = fwrite(buffer, sizeof(char), 80, outfile);
```

Returns

Both functions return the number of items actually read or written. If the return value is less than you expected, an error may have occurred. Call *ferror* to confirm.

See Also

```
read, write
```

Example

Lines 55 and 68 in Example 15-2 call *fread* and *fwrite*, respectively.

Stream I/O   **freopen** ◀

Purpose

Use *freopen* to close a file and open another file with the same file pointer. See *fopen* for more information on the function's arguments.

Syntax

```
#include <stdio.h>
FILE *freopen(const char *filename, const char *access_mode,
                                    FILE *stream);
```

const char *filename;	*Path name of file to be opened*
const char *access_mode;	*A character string denoting permissible operations (See Table 15-1.)*
FILE	*stream;	*Stream being reopened*

Example Call

```
freopen("output.txt", "w", stdout);
```

Returns

If all goes well, *freopen* returns a pointer to the newly opened file. Otherwise, it returns NULL.

See Also

fclose, fopen

▶ fscanf $\qquad$ *Stream I/O*

Purpose

Use the *fscanf* function to read characters from *stream*, convert them to values according to format specifications embedded in the argument *format_string* and finally store the values into C variables whose addresses are provided in the variable length argument list. See *scanf* for more details on the argument *format_string*.

Syntax

```
#include <stdio.h>
int fscanf(FILE *stream, const char *format_string,...);
FILE       *stream;               Stream from which reading occurs
const char *format_string;        Format to be used for output
...                               Variables being read
```

Example Call

```
fscanf(infile, "Date: %d/%d/%d", &month, &day, &year);
```

Returns

The *fscanf* function returns the number of input items that were successfully read, converted, and saved in the variable. If the file ends during I/O, EOF is returned.

See Also

cscanf, scanf, sscanf

▶ fseek, ftell $\qquad$ *Stream I/O*

Purpose

Use the *fseek* function to reposition *stream* to the location specified by *offset* with respect to the argument *origin*. The valid values of *origin* are the following constants: ·

fseek, ftell

SEEK_SET	Beginning of file
SEEK_CUR	Current position in the file
SEEK_END	End of file

On the other hand, use the *ftell* function to determine the current position in *stream*.

Syntax

```
#include <stdio.h>
int fseek(FILE *stream, long offset, int origin);
long ftell(FILE *stream);
FILE *stream;      Stream whose position is obtained or set
long offset;       Offset of new position (in bytes) from origin
int origin;        A constant indicating the position from which to offset
```

Example Call

```
fseek(infile, OL, SEEK_SET); /* Go to the beginning */
curpos = ftell(infile));
```

Returns

When successful, *fseek* returns 0, and *ftell* returns a long integer containing the byte offset of the current position in *stream*. In case of error, *fseek* returns a nonzero value and *ftell* returns −1L.

See Also

lseek, tell

Stream I/O   **getc, getchar** ◀

Purpose

Use the *getc* and *getchar* macros to read a single character from *stream* and from *stdin*, respectively.

Syntax

```
int getc(FILE *stream);
int getchar(void);
FILE *stream;      Stream from which a character is to read
```

Example Call

```
in_char = getc(p_txtfile);
c = getchar();
```

Returns

Both macros return the character read. In case of error, they return EOF.

See Also

fgetc, fgetchar, fputc, fputchar, putc, putchar

► gets
Stream I/O

Purpose

Use *gets* to read a line from the standard input file *stdin*, which is by default the keyboard.

Syntax

```
char *gets(char *buffer);
char     *buffer;      Buffer where string will be stored
```

Example Call

```
gets(command_line);
```

Returns

If successful, *gets* returns *buffer*. Otherwise, it returns NULL.

See Also

fgets, fputs, puts

Example

Lines 29 and 39 in Example 15-2 show calls to *gets*.

► getw, putw
Stream I/O

Purpose

Use *getw* and *putw*, respectively, to read from and write to *stream* a word (2 bytes) value.

Syntax

```
#include <stdio.h>
int getw(FILE *stream);
int putw(int intval, FILE *stream);
FILE *stream;      Stream on which I/O is done
int intval;        Integer to be written by putw
```

getw, putw

Example Call

```
word = getw(infile);
putw(0x1a, outfile); /* Write a Control-Z to outfile */
```

Returns

If successful, *getw* returns the integer it read, and *putw* returns the value it wrote. Otherwise, they return EOF, which is defined to be −1 in *stdio.h*. Since EOF is also a legitimate integer value, you should call *feof* and *ferror*, respectively, to determine if end-of-file was reached or if an error had occurred.

See Also

```
fread, read
```

Stream I/O   **printf ◄**

Purpose

Use *printf* to write character strings and values of C variables, formatted in a specified manner, to the standard output file *stdout*, normally the screen. The value of each argument is formatted according to the codes embedded in the string *format_string*. The format specification is of the following form:

```
%[Flags][Width].[Precision][Addressing_mode][Size][Type]
```

Table 15-3 summarizes each component of the format string. Tables 15-4 and 15-5 explain the *Flag* and the *Type* fields, respectively.

Table 15-3. The Fields in a *printf* Format Specification

Field	Explanation
Flags (optional)	One or more of the characters −, +, # or a blank space. (See Table 15-4.)
Width (optional)	A number to indicate how many characters, at a minimum, must be used to print the value.
Precision (optional)	Another number specifying how many characters, at most, can be used in printing the value. When printing integer variables, this is the minimum number of digits used.
Addressing_mode (optional)	This field is specific to Microsoft C. One of the letters F (for "far") or N (for "near") can be used to override the default addressing mode of the memory model being used.
Size (optional)	This is a character that modifies the *Type* field that comes next. The following characters may appear in this field:

Table 15-3. (cont.)

Field	Explanation	
	Prefix	*When to Use*
	h	Use when printing integers to indicate that the argument is a short integer.
	l	Use when printing integers or unsigned integers to indicate that the variable to be printed is a long integer.
	L	Use when the floating-point variable being printed is a long double.
Type (required)	A letter to indicate the type of variable being printed. (See Table 15-5.)	

Table 15-4. The *Flags* Field in the *printf* Format Specification

Flag	Meaning	Default
−	Left justify output value	Right justification.
+	If the output value is numerical, print a + or a − according to the sign of the value.	A negative sign (−) is printed for negative numerical values only.
space	Positive numerical values are prefixed with blank spaces.	No blanks are printed.
#	When used in printing integers in octal or hexadecimal, nonzero values are prefixed with 0, 0x, or 0X.	No special prefix appears.
	When printing floating point in %e, %E, or %f format, a decimal point is printed.	Decimal point appears only when digits follow it.
	For %g or %G formats, this flag prints a decimal point and also prints all trailing zeros.	Trailing zeros are truncated, and a decimal point appears only when digits follow.

Table 15-5. The *Type* Field in a *printf* Format Specification

Type	Type in C	Resulting Output Format
c	char	Single character. *printf("%c", 'Z');* prints a a Z.
d	int	Signed decimal integer as a sequence of digits with or without a sign depending on the *Flags* used. *printf("%d", 95);* prints 95.
e	double or float	Signed value in the scientific format, for example, −123.4567 is printed as −1.234567e+002.

printf

Table 15-5. (cont.)

Type	Type in C	Resulting Output Format
E	double or float	Signed value in the scientific format, the above example will print $-1.234567E+002$ if the %E format is used.
f	double or float	Signed value in the format, (sign)(digits).(digits), the example for %e will print -123.456700 if the %f format is used.
g	double or float	Signed value printed using one of %e or %f format. The format that generates the most compact output for the given "Precision" and value, is selected.
G	double or float	Signed value printed using the %g format, but with the letter G in place of e whenever exponents are printed.
i	int	Signed decimal integer as a sequence of digits with or without a sign depending on the *Flags* field.
n	Pointer to int	This is not really a printing format. The argument corresponding to this format is a pointer to an integer. Before returning, the *printf* function will store in this integer, the total number of characters it has printed.
o	unsigned	Octal digits without any sign.
p	far pointer to void	The address is printed in the form *SSSS:0000* where *SSSS* denotes the segment address and *0000* is the offset.
u	unsigned	Unsigned decimal integer as a sequence of digits.
x	unsigned	Hexadecimal digits using lowercase letters, *abcdef*.
X	unsigned	Hexadecimal digits using uppercase letters, *ABCDEF*.

Syntax

```
#include <stdio.h>
int printf(const char *format_string,...);
const char *format_string;        Format to be used for output
...                               Variables being printed
```

Example Call

```
printf("The product of %d and %d is %d\n", x, y, x*y);
```

Returns

The *printf* function returns the number of characters it has printed.

printf

See Also

cprintf, fprintf, sprintf, vfprintf, vprintf, vsprintf

Example

Examples 15-1 and 15-2 use *printf* for output.

▶ putc, putchar $\qquad$ *Stream I/O*

Purpose

Use the *putc* and *putchar* macros to write the character *c* to *stream* and to *stdout*, respectively.

Syntax

```
#include <stdio.h>
int putc(int c, FILE *stream);
int putchar(int c);
int  c;          Character to be written
FILE *stream;    Stream to which putc writes the character
```

Example Call

```
putc('*', outfile);
putchar('?');
```

Returns

Both macros return the character written. In case of any error, the constant EOF is returned. Call *ferror* to confirm the error.

See Also

fgetc, fgetchar, fputc, fputc, getc, getchar

▶ rewind $\qquad$ *Stream I/O*

Purpose

Use the *rewind* function to set the current read or write position of *stream* to the beginning of the file.

Syntax

```
#include <stdio.h>
void rewind(FILE *stream);
FILE    *stream;     Stream to be rewound
```

rewind

Example Call

rewind(input_file);

See Also

fseek, ftell, lseek, tell

Stream I/O **rmtmp** ◀

Purpose

Use *rmtmp* to close all temporary files opened by *tmpfile* and delete them from the current working directory.

Syntax

```
#include <stdio.h>
int rmtmp(void);
```

Example Call

num_removed = rmtmp();

Returns

The *rmtmp* function returns the total number of temporary files it closed and deleted.

See Also

tmpfile

Stream I/O **scanf** ◀

Purpose

Use *scanf* to read characters from the stream *stdin* and convert them to values of C variables according to format specified in the string *format_string*. The format specification for each variable has the following form:

%[*][Width][Addressing_mode][Size][Type]

Table 15-6 summarizes the purpose of each field in the format specification used by *scanf*. Further details are shown in Table 15-7.

Normally strings read using the %s format are assumed to be delimited by blank spaces. When you want to read a string delimited by any character other than those in a specific set, you can specify the set of characters within brackets and use this in place of the letter *s* in the format specification. On the other hand, if the first character inside the brackets is a caret (^), then the set is assumed to show the characters that terminate the string. Thus, for example, %[^'\"] will read a string delimited by single or double quote characters.

Table 15-6. The Fields in *scanf*'s Format Specification

Field	Explanation
% (required)	Indicates the beginning of a format specification. Use %% to read a percentage sign from the input.
* (optional)	The characters representing the value will be read according to the format specification, but the value will not be stored.
Width (optional)	A positive value specifying the maximum number of characters to be read for the value of this variable.
Addressing_mode (optional)	One of the letters F (for "far") or N (for "near") may be used to override the default addressing mode of the memory model being used.
Size (optional)	This is a character that modifies the *Type* field that comes next. One of the following characters may be used:

Prefix	When to Use
h	Use when reading integers to indicate that the argument is a short integer.
l	Use when reading integers or unsigned integers to specify that the variable whose value is being read is long. Also use with floating-point variables to indicate a double, rather than a float.

Field	Explanation
Type (required)	A letter to indicate the type of variable being read. (See Table 15-7.)

Table 15-7. The *Type* Field in Format Specification for *scanf*

Type	Expected Input	Type of Argument
c	Single character.	Pointer to char
d	Decimal integer.	Pointer to int
e,E, f, g,G	Signed value in the scientific format, for example, $-1.234567e+002$ and $9.876543e-002$.	Pointer to float
i	Decimal, hexadecimal, or octal integer.	Pointer to int
n	This is not really a reading format. The argument corresponding to this	Pointer to int

Table 15-7. (cont.)

Type	Expected Input	Type of Argument
	format is a pointer to an integer. Before returning, the *scanf* function will store, in this integer, the total number of characters it has read.	
o	Octal digits without any sign.	Pointer to int
p	Hexadecimal digits in the form *SSSS:OOOO* using uppercase letters.	Pointer to a far data pointer
s	Character string.	Pointer to an array of characters
u	Unsigned decimal integer.	Pointer to unsigned int
U	Unsigned decimal integer.	Pointer to unsigned long
x	Hexadecimal digits.	Pointer to int

Syntax

```
#include <stdio.h>
int scanf(const char *format_string,...);
const char *format_string;     Format to be used for input
...                            Variables being read
```

Example Call

```
scanf(" %d:%d:%d", &hour, &minute, &second);
```

Returns

The *scanf* function returns the number of input items that were successfully read, converted, and saved in variables. If file ends during reading, *scanf* returns EOF.

See Also

```
cscanf, fscanf, sscanf
```

Stream I/O   **setbuf, setvbuf ◄**

Purpose

Use the *setbuf* function to assign your own buffer instead of the system-allocated one for use by the file *stream*. The *setvbuf* function provides further control of buffering. It assigns a *buffer* of size *buf_size* to *stream*, which has been opened, but no I/O has been performed yet. The type of buffering is controlled by *buf_mode*. If *buf_mode* is _IOFBF, the I/O operations with the stream will be fully buffered. If it is _IOLBF, buffering will be done one line at a time. Setting *buf_mode* to _IONBF causes I/O to be unbuffered.

Syntax

```
#include <stdio.h>
void setbuf(FILE *stream, char *buffer);
int setvbuf(FILE *stream, char *buffer, int buf_mode,
                                        size_t buf_size);
```

FILE *stream;	*Stream being buffered*
char *buffer;	*Pointer to buffer, BUFSIZ bytes long for* setbuf *(or NULL if no buffering requested)*
int buf_mode;	*Type of buffering desired*
size_t buf_size;	*Size of buffer in bytes, if any assigned (for* setvbuf*)*

Example Call

```
setbuf(infile, mybuffer);
setvbuf(infile, buffer, _IOFBF, 120);
```

Returns

If successful, *setvbuf* returns zero. In case of any error, it returns a nonzero value.

---

 sprintf   *Stream I/O*

Purpose

Use the *sprintf* function to format and write the values of C variables to a string. See *printf* for a description of *format_string*.

Syntax

```
#include <stdio.h>
int sprintf(char *p_string, const char *format_string,...);
char      *p_string;        String to which output goes
const char *format_string;  Format to be used for output
...                         Variables being printed
```

Example Call

```
sprintf(buffer, "FY 88 Profit = %.2f\n", profit);
```

Returns

The *sprintf* function returns the number of characters it has stored in the buffer, excluding the terminating null character (\0).

See Also

```
fprintf, printf, vfprintf, vprintf, vsprintf
```

Example

Line 50 in Example 15-1 uses *sprintf* to prepare a string for output to a file.

sprintf

Stream I/O   **sscanf** ◄

Purpose

Use *sscanf* to read characters from a buffer and convert and store them in C variables according to specified formats. See *scanf* for a detailed description of *format_string*.

Syntax

```
#include <stdio.h>
int sscanf(const char *buffer, const char *format_string,...);
const char *buffer;              String from which sscanf reads
const char *format_string;       Format to be used for input
...                              Variables being read
```

Example Call

```
sscanf(buffer, "Name: %s Age: %d", name, &age);
```

Returns

The *sscanf* function returns the number of fields that were successfully read, converted, and assigned to variables. If the string ends before completing the read operation, *sscanf* will return EOF.

See Also

cscanf, fscanf, scanf

Stream I/O   **tempnam** ◄

Purpose

Use the *tempnam* function to generate a temporary file name for your application. The file name uses the default directory name from the MS-DOS environment variable TMP, if it is defined, and has the prefix specified by the argument *file_prefix*.

Syntax

```
#include <stdio.h>
char *tempnam(char *dir_name, char *file_prefix);
char *dir_name;         Pointer to string with directory name to be used if
                        the environment variable TMP is undefined
char *file_prefix;      Pointer to string with prefix characters for file
                        name
```

Example Call

```
tfilename = tempnam(NULL, "mceg");
```

Returns

The *tempnam* function returns a pointer to the name generated. If it cannot generate a unique name, it returns a NULL.

See Also

```
tmpfile, tmpnam
```

► tmpfile
Stream I/O

Purpose

Use *tmpfile* to open a temporary file in the current directory for buffered binary read/write operations ("wb+" mode).

Syntax

```
#include <stdio.h>
FILE *tmpfile(void);
```

Example Call

```
p_tfile = tmpfile();
```

Returns

If successful, *tmpfile* returns a pointer to the stream. Otherwise, it returns NULL.

See Also

```
rmtmp, tempnam, tmpnam
```

► tmpnam
Stream I/O

Purpose

Use the *tmpnam* function to generate a temporary file name in the string *file_name*, which must have enough room to hold at least *L_tmpnam* (a constant defined in *stdio.h*) characters. You can generate up to *TMP_MAX* (another constant defined in *stdio.h*) unique file names.

Syntax

```
#include <stdio.h>
```

tmpnam

```
char *tmpnam(char *file_name);
char      *file_name;       Pointer to string where file name will be
                            returned
```

Example Call

```
char tfilename[L_tmpnam];
tmpnam(tfilename);
```

Returns

If successful, *tmpnam* returns *file_name*. If the generated name is not unique, it returns NULL.

See Also

```
tempnam, tmpfile
```

Stream I/O **ungetc** ◄

Purpose

Use *ungetc* to push the character *c* into the buffer associated with *stream*. You can push any character except the constant EOF.

Syntax

```
#include <stdio.h>
int ungetc(int c, FILE *stream);
int c;             Character to be pushed back
FILE *stream;      Stream where character goes
```

Example Call

```
ungetc(last_char, infile);
```

Returns

If there are no errors, *ungetc* returns the character it pushed back. Otherwise, it returns EOF.

See Also

```
getc, getchar, putc, putchar
```

Stream I/O **vfprintf, vprintf, vsprintf** ◄

Purpose

Use *vfprintf* to write formatted output to a file, just as *fprintf* does, except that *vfprintf* accepts a pointer to the list of variables rather than the variables themselves, allowing a variable number of items to be printed. The *vprintf* and *vsprintf* behave similarly and are variable-argument counterparts of the functions *printf* and *sprintf*, respectively. See *printf* for a detailed description of the *format_string* argument.

Syntax

```
#include <stdarg.h>
#include <stdio.h>
int vfprintf(FILE *stream, const char *format_string,
                                    va_list arg_pointer);
int vprintf(const char *format_string, va_list arg_pointer);
int vsprintf(char *p_string, const char *format_string,
                                    va_list arg_pointer);
```

FILE	*stream;	*Stream where output goes*
char	*p_string;	*String to which* vsprintf *writes*
const char	*format_string;	*Format to be used for output*
va_list	arg_pointer;	*Variables being printed*

Example Call

```
vfprintf(stderr, p_format, p_arg);
```

Returns

Each function returns the number of characters it has printed, excluding the terminating null character (\0).

See Also

```
cprintf, fprintf, printf, sprintf, va_start, va_arg, va_end
```

Example

Example 15-3 shows how *vfprintf* can be used to write a custom error handler.

► **close**   *Low-Level I/O*

Purpose

Use *close* to close a file.

Syntax

```
#include <io.h>
int close(int handle);
int handle;      Handle of open file to be closed
```

Example Call

```
close(handle);
```

close

Returns

If successful, *close* returns 0. Otherwise, it returns a −1 to indicate error and sets *errno* to an error code.

See Also

fclose, fopen, open

Low-Level I/O   **creat**

Purpose

Use *creat* to create a new file or truncate an existing file. See *open* for more on *pmode*.

Syntax

```
#include <io.h>
#include <sys\types.h>
#include <sys\stat.h>
int creat(char *filename, int pmode);
char *filename;          Path name of file to be opened
int pmode;               Read/write permission settings
```

Example Call

```
handle = creat("temp.dat", S_IREAD|S_IWRITE);
```

Returns

If the file is successfully created (or truncated), *creat* returns a valid handle to the file. Otherwise, it returns −1 and sets *errno* to an error code.

See Also

open, umask

Low-Level I/O   **dup, dup2** ◄

Purpose

Use *dup* to create a second handle for a file that is already open. Use *dup2* to force a second handle to refer to the same file as the first one.

Syntax

```
#include <io.h>
int dup(int handle1);
```

```
int dup2(int handle1, int handle2);
int handle1;        Handle of an open file
int handle2;        Another handle that dup2 will associate with the same file
                    as handle1
```

Example Call

```
new_handle = dup(old_handle);
```

Returns

If a new handle is successfully created, *dup* returns the duplicate handle. If *dup2* is successful, it returns 0. In case of error, both routines return −1 and set *errno* to an error code.

See Also

```
creat, open
```

---

 eof   *Low-Level I/O*

Purpose

Use the *eof* function to determine whether end-of-file has been reached on a file.

Syntax

```
#include <io.h>
int eof(int handle);
int handle;        Handle of an open file
```

Example Call

```
if(eof(handle) != 0) printf("File ended!\n");
```

Returns

For a valid file handle, *eof* returns 1 to indicate an end-of-file and 0 when it's not. Otherwise, it returns −1 and sets *errno* to EBADF.

See Also

```
feof, ferror
```

 **lseek, tell**   *Low-Level I/O*

Purpose

Use *lseek* to move to a new position in a file. See *fseek* for a list of

lseek, tell

values that *origin* can take. You can use *tell* to determine the current position in a file.

Syntax

```
#include <stdio.h>
#include <io.h>
long lseek(int handle, long offset, int origin);
long tell(int handle);
int handle;       File handle
long offset;      Offset of new position (in bytes) from origin
int origin;       A constant indicating the position from which to offset
```

Example Call

```
newpos = lseek(fhandle, 512L, SEEK_SET); /* Skip 512 bytes */
curpos = tell(filehandle);
```

Returns

When successful, both functions return the offset of the current position from the beginning of the file. In case of error, they return −1 and set *errno* to an error code.

See Also

```
fseek, ftell
```

Low-Level I/O   **open ◀**

Purpose

Use the *open* function to open the file named *filename*. The argument *oflag* specifies the operations you intend to perform on the file after opening. Use bitwise-OR of constants from Table 15-8 to specify *oflag*.

Table 15-8. List of Constants Indicating Type of Operations Allowed on File

Constant	Interpretation of the Constant
O_APPEND	Writing will always occur at the end of the file.
O_BINARY	File is opened in the binary or untranslated mode. This is the same as the binary (b) mode used with *fopen*, see *fopen* for explanation.
O_CREAT	Creates and opens a file for writing if the named file does not exist.
O_EXCL	Returns an error value if file already exists and O_CREAT was specified.
O_RDONLY	File is opened for reading only. When O_RDONLY is given, O_WRONLY and O_RDWR are disallowed.

Table 15-8. (cont.)

Constant	Interpretation of the Constant
O_RDWR	File is opened for both reading and writing. When O_RDWR is given, O_RDONLY and O_WRONLY are disallowed.
O_TEXT	File is opened in text or translated mode. This is the same text mode used with *fopen*. See *fopen* for elaboration.
O_TRUNC	Opens an existing file and truncates it to zero length, destroying its current contents.
O_WRONLY	File is opened for writing only. When O_WRONLY is used, O_RDONLY and O_RDWR are not allowed.

The third argument to *open*, *pmode*, is necessary only when requesting the creation of a new file by using the flag O_CREAT. The value in *pmode* will be used in setting the permission of the newly created file. Table 15-9 shows the possible values. These constants are defined in the header file *sys\stat.h*.

Table 15-9. Permission Settings for Newly Created Files

Constant	Interpretation of the Constant
S_IWRITE	Both reading and writing permitted.
S_IREAD	Only reading permitted.
S_IREAD | S_IWRITE	Both reading and writing permitted.

The *sopen* function is similar to *open*, but it takes an additional argument *shflag*, which allows you to open a file for shared access (provided you are using MS-DOS 3.0 and later and you enable sharing by the DOS command SHARE). The argument *shflag* should be specified by bitwise OR of an appropriate combination of constants defined in the file *share.h* and shown in Table 15-10.

Table 15-10. List of Constants to Indicate the Level of File Sharing

Constant	Interpretation of Constant
SH_COMPAT	No other process will be allowed to access the file.
SH_DENYRW	A single process has exclusive read and write access to the file.
SH_DENYWR	No other process can access the file for writing.
SH_DENYRD	No other process can access the file for reading.
SH_DENYNO	Any process may access the file for both reading and for writing.

open

Syntax

```
#include <io.h>
#include <share.h>    /* Only for sopen */
#include <fcntl.h>
#include <sys\types.h>
#include <sys\stat.h>
int open(char *filename, int oflag [, int pmode]);
int sopen(char *filename, int oflag, int shflag [, int pmode])
                                                               ;

char *filename;     Path name of file to be opened
int oflag;          Operations allowed on file
int shflag;         Sharing mode (See Table 15-10.)
int pmode;          An optional argument to specify read/write
                    permission of a new file
```

Example Call

```
filehandle = open("temp.dat", O_WRONLY|O_CREAT, S_IWRITE);
fhandle = sopen("c:\\autoexec.bat", O_RDONLY, SH_DENYRW);
```

Returns

If successful, both functions return the file handle. Otherwise, they return −1 and set *errno* to an error code.

See Also

close, fopen

Low-Level I/O   **read, write** ◀

Purpose

Use *read* to read *count* bytes from a file to *buffer*. The reading from the file begins at the current position, which is appropriately incremented afterward. The *write* function is for writing from a buffer to a file.

Syntax

```
#include <io.h>
int read(int handle, void *buffer, unsigned count);
int write(int handle, void *buffer, unsigned count);
int handle;         Handle of file with which I/O occurs
char *buffer;       Pointer to buffer used in I/O
unsigned count;     Number of bytes to be read or written
```

Example Call

```
read(handle, data_buffer, 1024);
write(handle, data_buffer, 1024);
```

read, write

Returns

Both functions return the number of bytes actually read from or written to the file. In case of any error, they return −1 and set *errno* to an error code.

See Also

creat, open, sopen

 **cgets, cputs** *Console and Port I/O*

Purpose

Use *cgets* and *cputs*, respectively, to read from and write to the console a string. On input, you should set *inbuf[0]* to the maximum number of characters to be read. The actual number read will be returned by *cgets* in *inbuf[1]*.

Syntax

```
#include <conio.h>
char *cgets(char *inbuf);
int cputs(char *outbuf);
char       *inbuf;      Buffer where string will be stored
const char *outbuf;     Null-terminated string to be output
```

Example Call

```
cgets(user_input);
cputs("Are you sure (Y/N)? ");
```

Returns

The *cgets* function returns a pointer to the beginning of the string, i.e., the location *inbuf[2]* and *cputs* returns 0 (in versions prior to 5.0, *cputs* has no return value).

See Also

gets, puts

► **cprintf, cscanf** *Console and Port I/O*

Purpose

Use *cprintf* for formatted output to the console. The *cscanf* function is for input. See *printf* and *scanf* for details of the format specification, respectively. Note that unlike the *fprintf*,

cprintf, cscanf

printf, and *sprintf* functions, *cprintf* does not translate newlines (\n) to CR-LF (\r\n). You have to use CR-LF (\r \n) explicitly to go to the beginning of the next line.

Syntax

```
#include <conio.h>
int cprintf(const char *format_string, ...);
int cscanf(const char *format_string, ...);
const char *format_string;   Formatting codes for input and output
...                          Variables being printed or read
```

Example Call

```
cprintf("File %s has %d bytes of data\r\n", fname, size);
cscanf(" %d/%d/%d", &month, &day, &year);
```

Returns

The *cprintf* function returns the number of characters it has printed on the console while *cscanf* returns the number of fields that were successfully read, converted, and assigned to variables.

See Also

fprintf, printf, sprintf

Console and Port I/O   **getch, getche** ◀

Purpose

Use the *getch* function to read a character from the keyboard without echoing it back to the display. The *getche* function performs the same task, but it echoes the character.

Syntax

```
#include <conio.h>
int getch(void);
```

Example Call

```
in_char = getch();
```

Returns

Each function returns the character read from the keyboard.

See Also

fgetc, getc, getchar

inp, inpw *Console and Port I/O*

Purpose

Use *inp* and *inpw* to read a byte and a word from the I/O port *portid*, respectively.

Syntax

```
#include <conio.h>
int inp(unsigned portid);
unsigned int inpw(unsigned portid);
unsigned portid;        Port address for input
```

Example Call

```
byte_read = inp(0x3f8);
word_8259 = inpw(0x20);
```

Returns

Each function returns the data read from the port.

See Also

```
outp, outpw
```

Example

Lines 18 and 36 in Example 15-4 use *inp* to read from an I/O port on the Intel 8255 chip in an IBM PC.

▶ kbhit *Console and Port I/O*

Purpose

Use the console I/O function *kbhit* to check if any keystrokes are waiting to be read.

Syntax

```
#include <conio.h>
int kbhit(void);
```

Example Call

```
/* Do your thing until user presses a key */
        while( !kbhit() ) do_your_thing();
```

kbhit

Returns

If a key is pressed, *kbhit* returns a nonzero value. Otherwise, it returns zero.

See Also

_bios_keybrd

Console and Port I/O   **outp, outpw** ◀

Purpose

Use *outp* and *outpw* to write a byte and a word to the I/O port *portid*, respectively.

Syntax

```
#include <conio.h>
int outp(unsigned portid, int byte_value);
unsigned outpw(unsigned portid, unsigned word_value);
unsigned portid;          I/O port address
int byte_value;           Byte to be written to the port
unsigned word_value;      Word to be written to the port
```

Example Call

```
outpw(0x3ce, (2<<8) | 0x5); /* Put EGA in write mode 2 */
outp(0x43, 0xb6);  /* Use the timer chip as oscillator */
```

See Also

inp, inpw

Example

Example 15-4 shows how *outp* is used to control the speaker in an IBM PC.

Console and Port I/O   **putch** ◀

Purpose

Use the *putch* function to write a single character to the display without any intermediate buffering.

Syntax

```
#include <conio.h>
int putch(int c);
int c;      Character to be written
```

putch

Example Call

```
putch('>');
```

Returns

When successful, *putch* returns the character it wrote. Otherwise, it returns EOF.

See Also

```
getch, getche
```

► ungetch *Console and Port I/O*

Purpose

Use the *ungetch* function to push a single character back to the keyboard buffer. This character will be the next character read from the console.

Syntax

```
#include <conio.h>
int ungetch(int c);
int c;      Character to be pushed back into the keyboard buffer
```

Example Call

```
ungetch(last_char);
```

Returns

If successful, *ungetch* returns the character it pushed back. Otherwise, it returns EOF to indicate an error, which is why you should not try to push back EOF.

See Also

```
getch, getche
```

Example 15-1   While writing this guide, we needed a program to number the lines of the listings that appear in each example. The following program was used for this purpose. It opens a source file, reads a line, adds a line number, and writes it out to a destination file. This cycle is repeated until we reach end-of-file in the source file.

```
1:/* This program numbers the lines in a file.
2: * We assume a maximum of 999 lines in the file.
3: */
4:#include <stdio.h>
```

ungetch

```
 5:#define MAXCHR  80
 6:main()
 7:{
 8:    char line[MAXCHR], infilename[MAXCHR],
 9:         outfilename[MAXCHR], *rline;
10:    FILE *infile, *outfile;
11:    int lineno = 0;
12:    rline = &line[4];
13:    printf("Line numbering program\n"
14:           "Enter input file name:");
15:    gets(infilename);
16:/* Open input file in text mode for read
17: * operations
18: */
19:    if ((infile = fopen(infilename,"r")) == NULL)
20:    {
21:        printf("Error opening %s\n", infilename);
22:        exit(1);
23:    }
24:    printf("Enter output file name:");
25:    gets(outfilename);
26:/* Open output file in text mode for write
27: * operations
28: */
29:    if ((outfile = fopen(outfilename,"w")) == NULL)
30:    {
31:        printf("Error opening %s\n", outfilename);
32:        exit(1);
33:    }
34:/* Read lines from the input file, add line numbers
35: * and write each line out */
36:    while(1)
37:    {
38:        if(fgets(rline, MAXCHR, infile) == NULL)
39:        {
40:            if(ferror(infile) != 0)
41:                puts("Error during read");
42:            if(feof(infile) != 0)
43:                    puts("File ended");
44:            clearerr(infile);
45:            break; /* Exit the while loop */
46:        }
47:        else
48:        {
49:            lineno++;
50:            sprintf(line, "%3d", lineno);
51:            line[3] = ':';
52:            fputs(line, outfile);
53:        }
54:    }
55:    printf("%d lines written to %s\n",
56:            lineno, outfilename);
```

```
57:    fclose(infile);
58:    fclose(outfile);
59:}
```

Example 15-2   This program converts a WordStar document
to a plain text file. This can be accomplished
by stripping the eighth bit of each byte in the
WordStar document.

```
 1:/*  This program converts a WordStar file to a
 2: *  plain text file.
 3: */
 4:#include <stdio.h>
 5:#include <ctype.h>
 6:
 7:#define MAXCHR     80
 8:#define BLKSIZE    512
 9:
10:static unsigned char inbuf[BLKSIZE],
11:                     outbuf[BLKSIZE];
12:
13:/* Function prototype */
14:size_t process_block(unsigned char *ibuf,
15:                     unsigned char *obuf,
16:                     size_t numchar);
17:
18:main()
19:{
20:    char infilename[MAXCHR],
21:         outfilename[MAXCHR];
22:    long processed=0L, converted=0L;
23:    size_t numread, numconv;
24:    int alldone = 0;
25:    FILE *infile, *outfile;
26:
27:    printf("WordStar to Text..."
28:           "\nEnter input file name:");
29:    gets(infilename);
30:/* Open input file in binary mode for read
31: * operations
32: */
33:    if ((infile = fopen(infilename,"rb")) == NULL)
34:    {
35:        printf("Error opening %s\n", infilename);
36:        exit(1);
37:    }
38:    printf("Enter output file name:");
39:    gets(outfilename);
40:
41:/* Open output file in binary mode for write
42: * operations
43: */
44:    if ((outfile = fopen(outfilename,"wb+")) == NULL)
```

```
45:    {
46:        printf("Error opening %s\n", outfilename);
47:        exit(1);
48:    }
49:
50:/* Read 512-byte blocks from the input file, convert
51: * where necessary and write the block out
52: */
53:    while(1)
54:    {
55:        if((numread = fread(inbuf, sizeof(char), BLKSIZE,
56:                            infile)) < BLKSIZE)
57:        {
58:            if(ferror(infile) != 0)
59:                puts("Error during read");
60:            if(feof(infile) != 0)
61:                    puts("File ended");
62:            clearerr(infile);
63:            alldone = 1;
64:        }
65:        processed += numread;
66:/* Process this block */
67:        numconv = process_block(inbuf, outbuf, numread);
68:        if(fwrite(outbuf, sizeof(char),
69:                            numconv, outfile) < numconv)
70:        {
71:            if(ferror(outfile) != 0)
72:                puts("Error during write");
73:            if(feof(outfile) != 0)
74:                    puts("No more room, maybe?");
75:            clearerr(outfile);
76:            alldone = 1;
77:        }
78:        converted += numconv;
79:        if(alldone) break; /* Exit the while loop */
80:    }
81:    printf("\n%ld bytes from %s generated %ld bytes"
82:            "\nwhich were written to %s\n", processed,
83:            infilename, converted, outfilename);
84:
85:    fclose(infile);
86:    fclose(outfile);
87:}
88:/*--------------------------------------------------------*/
89:size_t process_block(unsigned char *ibuf,
90:                     unsigned char *obuf,
91:                     size_t numchar)
92:{
93:    size_t i, count;
94:    int c;
95:
96:    for(i=0, count=0; i < numchar; i++)
```

```
 97:   {
 98:        c = ibuf[i];
 99:/* Take out bit7 of each character */
100:        c &= 0x7f;
101:/* Retain CR LF */
102:        if(c == '\r' || c == '\n')
103:        {
104:             obuf[count] = c;
105:             count++;
106:             continue;
107:        }
108:/* Drop all other unprintable characters */
109:        if(isprint(c) != 0 )
110:        {
111:             obuf[count] = c;
112:             count++;
113:             continue;
114:        }
115:   }
116:   return(count);
117:}
```

Example 15-3   This example shows an error-handling rou-
                  tine that takes a variable number of argu-
                  ments and prints an error message to the
                  predefined stream *stderr*. The arguments are
                  extracted by the macros *va_start*, *va_arg*,
                  and *va_end*, which are defined in *stdarg.h*.
                  The printing is done by *vfprintf*. A sample
                  main program is included.

```
 1:#include <stdio.h>
 2:#include <stdarg.h>
 3:void error_handler(char *,...);
 4:char filename[80] = "[5]Example.C";
 5:main()
 6:{
 7:        int line_no = 31;
 8:/* Call the error handler to print an error message.
 9: * First just a single line. Then a more detailed message
10: * with more arguments.
11: */
12:        error_handler("Syntax error\n");
13:        error_handler("File: %s at line: %d\n", filename,
14:                        line_no);
15:}
16:/*-------------------------------------------------------*/
17:/*  error_handler: accepts variable number of arguments
18: *                 and prints messages to stderr
19: */
20:void error_handler(char *my_format,...)
21:{
22:    va_list arg_pointer;
```

```
23:/* Use va_start macro to get to the start of the variable
24: * number of arguments. This will alter the pointer
25: * arg_pointer to point to the list of variables to be
26: * printed.
27: */
28:    va_start(arg_pointer, my_format);
29:    vfprintf(stderr, my_format, arg_pointer);
30:/* Use the va_end macro to reset the arg_pointer        */
31:    va_end(arg_pointer);
32:}
33:
```

Example 15-4   The IBM PC's speaker can be used to generate a tone by programming it via the 8255 chip at port address 61h and using the system timer (Intel 8254 chip) to control the speaker. Essentially, the steps involved follow. First, you will set up the timer as an oscillator by sending the data byte B6h to the port 43h. Then you compute the ratio of the frequency of sound you want and the frequency of the timer's clock frequency (1.19 MHz). Write this to port 42h. Tell the 8255 chip to drive the speaker under the control of the timer by reading from the port 61h and writing the value back with the first two bits set to 1 (perform a bitwise-OR with 3). This gets the sound going. Let the sound continue as long as you wish. Shut the speaker off by reading port 61h again and setting bits 0 and 1 to zero.

```
1:#include <conio.h>
2:
3:#define TIMER_FREQ  1193180L /* Timer freq = 1.19 MHz */
4:#define TIMER_COUNT 0x42 /* 8253 timer -- count        */
5:#define TIMER_MODE  0x43 /* 8253 timer control port    */
6:#define TIMER_OSC   0xb6 /*To use timer as oscillator */
7:#define OUT_8255    0x61 /* 8255 PPI output port adrs */
8:#define SPKRON      3 /* Bit 0 = control spkr by timer*/
9:                      /* Bit 1 = speaker on/off        */
10:main()
11:{
12:    unsigned freq, status, ratio, part_ratio;
13:    char input[81];
14:    cprintf("Enter frequency in Hz \
15:(between 100 and 15000):");
16:    cscanf("%hu", &freq);
17:/* First read and save status of the 8255 chip */
18:    status = inp (OUT_8255);
19:/* Put timer in oscillator mode */
20:    outp (TIMER_MODE, TIMER_OSC);
21:        ratio = (unsigned)(TIMER_FREQ/freq);
22:    part_ratio = ratio & 0xff; /* low byte of ratio    */
```

```
23:     outp(TIMER_COUNT, part_ratio);
24:     part_ratio = (ratio >> 8) & 0xff; /* high byte    */
25:     outp(TIMER_COUNT, part_ratio);
26:/* Finally turn on speaker */
27:     outp (OUT_8255, (status | SPKRON));
28:
29:/* Ask user to indicate when to stop the
30: * annoying tone...
31: */
32:         cprintf("\nHit return to exit:");
33:         cgets(input);
34:
35:/* Now turn off speaker */
36:     status = inp (OUT_8255); /* get current status */
37:/* Turn speaker off */
38:     outp (OUT_8255, (status & ~SPKRON));
39:}
```

16
System Calls

All IBM-compatible PCs come with a basic input/output system (BIOS) built into the system's read-only memory (ROM). The BIOS is a set of low-level I/O routines for accessing peripheral devices such as the keyboard, display, printer, serial port, and floppy or hard disk. In addition to the built-in ROM BIOS, MS-DOS itself has a host of standard utility functions that also perform I/O and provide access to the DOS file system. The Microsoft C library includes a set of functions that provide access to the BIOS and DOS services from your C programs. These functions for making "system calls" enable you to harness the full potential of the PC without having to write, in many cases, even a single line of code in 8086 assembly language.

The number of system features and peripherals that you can access and manipulate using this set of routines is quite large. The limited space in this guide precludes the possibility of any detailed discussion of all the things you can do with these routines. Therefore, you should consult a comprehensive reference book such as *The Waite Group's Microsoft C Bible* for further details on these routines and for many more examples of their use.

► bdos

Purpose

Use the *bdos* function to call a subset of the DOS functions that can be invoked by an INT 21h instruction. You can use *bdos* to call only those DOS functions that require no arguments or that take arguments in the DX and the AL registers only. In contrast to the more general purpose *intdos* and *intdosx*, the *bdos* function is a simplified way to access a small set of DOS functions.

Syntax

```
#include <dos.h>
int bdos (int funcno, unsigned dx_val, unsigned al_val);
int funcno;           DOS function number
unsigned dx_val;      DX register value
unsigned al_val;      AL register value
```

Example Call

```
bdos(2, q', 0); /* Use DOS function 2 to display 'q' */
```

Returns

The return value is the content of the *AX* register at the end of the DOS call. For example, if the DOS call returns a value in *AL*, you can get this value by ignoring the high-order byte of the return value.

See Also

```
intdos, intdosx
```

► __bios__disk

Purpose

Use the *__bios__disk* function to perform raw disk I/O operations on the PC's diskette and hard disk drives by using the BIOS disk services available via interrupt 13h. Since this function allows you to perform low-level disk I/O directly, you should use it with caution because it can destroy data and damage the MS-DOS file system that may already exist on your disk. Use one of the constants _DISK_RESET, _DISK_STATUS, _DISK_READ, _DISK_WRITE, _DISK_VERIFY, or _DISK_FORMAT to specify the service to be performed by *__bios__disk*. The *diskinfo_t* structure declared in *bios.h* and shown below is used to hold information about the disk drive.

__bios__disk

```
struct diskinfo_t
{
    unsigned drive;      /* Drive number (0 for first
                            floppy drive, 1 for second,
                            80 for first hard disk,
                            81 for the second one, and so on*/
    unsigned head;       /* Head number or which side?   */
    unsigned track;      /* Track number                 */
    unsigned sector;     /* Start sector number          */
    unsigned nsectors;   /* Number of sectors for which
                            service is performed          */
    void far *buffer;    /* Pointer to buffer for use
                            during requested service      */
};
```

Consult *The Waite Group's Microsoft C Bible* for further information on using the *_bios_disk* function.

Syntax

```
#include <bios.h>
unsigned _bios_disk (unsigned service, struct diskinfo_t
                                                    *info);
```

unsigned service;   *Service code*
struct diskinfo_t *info;   *Pointer to structure to hold disk*
                               information

Example Call

```
_bios_disk(_DISK_READ, &info);
```

Returns

The *_bios_disk* function always returns the contents of the *AX* register at the end of the call.

See Also

int86, int86x

__bios__equiplist ◄

Purpose

Use *_bios_equiplist* to get information about the hardware and peripherals in the user's PC by using BIOS interrupt 11h.

Syntax

```
#include <bios.h>
unsigned _bios_equiplist (void);
```

Example Call

```
equip_flag = _bios_equiplist();
```

Returns

The *_bios_equip* function returns an unsigned 16-bit value, which should be interpreted as shown in Table 16-1. Note that bit 0 is the least significant bit.

Table 16-1. Meaning of Bits in Value Returned by
_bios_equiplist

Bits	Meaning
0	1 = one or more disk drives attached, 0 = no disk drives.
1	1 = a math coprocessor is present, 0 = no.
2–3	Size of system memory in units of 4K.
4–5	Initial video mode (00 = unused, 01 = 40x25 black and white text with color card, 10 = 80x25 black and white text with color card, 11 = 80x25 text on monochrome card).
6–7	Number of disk drives installed (00 = 1, 01 = 2). Only floppy disk drives are reported.
8	Set to 0 only if a DMA (Direct Memory Access) chip is present.
9–11	Number of RS 232C serial ports in the system.
12	1 = a game adapter is installed.
13	1 = a serial printer is attached.
14–15	Number of printers attached to system.

See Also

int86, int86x

► __bios__keybrd

Purpose

Use *_bios_keybrd* to access the BIOS routines for keyboard I/O by using interrupt 16h. You can use it to read the next available character, to check if a character is waiting to be read, and to check if the special keys such as Alt, Ctrl, and shift are being pressed. Table 16-2 shows the constants that are used to specify a service to be performed by *_bios_keybrd*.

Table 16-2. List of Services Offered by *_bios_keybrd*

Service Name	Service Performed
_KEYBRD_READ	Reads next available character from the keyboard buffer.
_KEYBRD_READY	Checks the keyboard buffer for characters waiting to be read.
_KEYBRD_SHIFTSTATUS	Returns current status of the shift, Ctrl, and Alt keys, and whether the Scroll

Table 16-2. (cont.)

Service Name	Service Performed
	Lock, Num Lock, and Caps Lock indicators are on.

Syntax

```
#include <bios.h>
unsigned _bios_keybrd (unsigned service);
unsigned service;    Keyboard function requested
```

Example Call

```
ch_read = _bios_keybrd(_KEYBRD_READ) & 0xff;
```

Returns

After the call *_bios_keybrd(_KEYBRD_READ)*, the low-order byte of the return value contains the ASCII code of the character just read, the high-order byte has the *scan code*, which is a unique byte generated by the keyboard whenever a key is either pressed or released. (See *The Waite Group's Microsoft C Bible* for further information.) For the _KEYBRD_SHIFTSTATUS service, the return value should be interpreted by consulting Table 16-3.

Table 16-3. Interpreting the SHIFT Status Byte Returned by
_bios_keybrd

Bit	Interpretation When Bit Is 1
0	Rightmost shift key pressed.
1	Leftmost shift key pressed.
2	Ctrl key pressed.
3	Alt key pressed.
4	Scroll Lock indicator is on.
5	Num Lock indicator is on.
6	Caps Lock indicator is on.
7	In insert mode.

See Also

getch, int86, kbhit

__bios__memsize

Purpose

Use *_bios_memsize* to generate interrupt 12h that returns the amount of memory in the PC. A program can use this to check if there is enough memory for it to run.

Syntax

```
#include <bios.h>
unsigned _bios_memsize (void);
```

Example Call

```
total_kilobytes = _bios_memsize();
```

Returns

The return value is the total memory in the system in 1K (1024 bytes) blocks.

► __bios__printer

Purpose

Use *_bios_printer* to access the BIOS interrupt 17h that lets you communicate with the printer. You can initialize the printer, determine its status, and send characters to the printer using this function. Use the constants _PRINTER_STATUS, _PRINTER_INIT, and _PRINTER_WRITE to specify the service.

Syntax

```
#include <bios.h>
unsigned _bios_printer (unsigned service,
                        unsigned printer, unsigned data);
unsigned service;        Printer function requested
unsigned printer;        Printer port, 0=LPT1:, 1=LPT2:
unsigned data;           Character being sent to printer
```

Example Call

```
_bios_printer(_PRINTER_WRITE, LPT1, 'x');
```

Returns

The low-order byte of the return value represents the status of the printer. The meaning of the bits are shown in Table 16-4.

Table 16-4. Interpreting the Status Byte of the Printer

Bit	Interpretation When Bit Is 1
0	Printer has timed out.
1	Not used.
2	Not used.
3	I/O error has occurred.
4	Printer is selected for output.
5	Printer is out of paper.

Table 16-4. (cont.)

Bit	Interpretation When Bit Is 1
6	Acknowledgment from printer.
7	Printer not busy. (If bit is 0, printer is busy.)

See Also

int86, int86x

__bios__serialcom ◄

Purpose

Use _bios_serialcom to access the RS232 serial ports of the PC and use the services offered by BIOS interrupt 14h. You can use this function to perform "polled" I/O, set communications parameters (e.g., baud rate and parity) and check the status of the port. Use the constants _COM_INIT, _COM_SEND, _COM_RECEIVE, and _COM_STATUS to specify the service to be performed by _bios_serialcom. It is simple to specify the communications parameters: Pick one constant from each of the four categories shown in Table 16-5 and OR them together to construct the unsigned argument *data*.

Table 16-5. Constants for Selecting Communications Parameters

Category Name	List of Constants	Communications Parameter Setting
Word length	_COM_CHR7	7 bits per character
	_COM_CHR8	8 bits per character
Stop bits	_COM_STOP1	1 stop bit
	_COM_STOP2	2 stop bits
Parity	_COM_NOPARITY	No parity bit
	_COM_EVENPARITY	Even parity
	_COM_ODDPARITY	Odd parity
Baud rate	_COM_110	110 baud
	_COM_150	150 baud
	_COM_300	300 baud
	_COM_600	600 baud
	_COM_1200	1200 baud
	_COM_2400	2400 baud
	_COM_4800	4800 baud
	_COM_9600	9600 baud

For example, if you select 8 bit word length, 1 stop bit, no parity, and a baud rate of 300 baud, use

```
(_COM_CHR8 | _COM_STOP1 | _COM_NOPARITY | _COM_300)
```

as the *data* argument with the service code _COM_INIT.

Syntax

```
#include <bios.h>
unsigned _bios_serialcom (unsigned service, unsigned port,
                                            unsigned data);
unsigned service;     Service requested
unsigned port;        Serial port number, 0=COM1, 1=COM1
unsigned data;        Character to be sent or communications parameters
```

Example Call

```
ch_rcvd = 0xff & _bios_serialcom(_COM_RECEIVE, COM1, 0);
```

Returns

The high-order byte of the return value always represents the status of the communications port. When reading a character from the serial port using the _COM_RECEIVE service, the low-order byte of the return value is the character just read, provided that none of the bits in the high-order byte is set. If any bit in the high-order byte is set, an error has occurred and the cause of the error is indicated by the bit that is set. (Consult *The Waite Group's Microsoft C Bible* for further details.)

See Also

int86, int86x

Example

Example 16-1 shows a simple communications program based on _bios_serialcom.

► **_bios_timeofday**

Purpose

Use the _bios_timeofday function to retrieve or set the current system clock count on the PC. This function is a gateway to the services offered by BIOS interrupt 1Ah. Use one of the constants _TIME_GETCLOCK or _TIME_SETCLOCK as the *service* argument.

Syntax

```
#include <bios.h>
unsigned _bios_timeofday (unsigned service, long *clockcount);
unsigned service;     Service requested
long     *clockcount; Timer clock counts
```

Example Call

```
_bios_timeofday(_TIME_GETCLOCK, &clock_count);
```

Returns

The return value is defined only when *service* is _TIME_GET-CLOCK. In this case, a return value of 1 indicates that midnight has passed since the last time the clock was read.

See Also

```
_dos_gettime, _dos_settime, int86, int86x
```

__chain__intr ◄

Purpose

Use _*chain_intr* to jump from one interrupt handler to another. You can, for example, write your own interrupt handler for a particular interrupt. After performing the tasks you want done, you can call _*chain_intr* to jump to the interrupt handler originally installed.

Syntax

```
#include <dos.h>
void _chain_intr (void (interrupt far *handler)());
interrupt far *handler;        Far pointer to the handler, a function of
                               type interrupt
```

Example Call

```
void (interrupt far *old_handler)();
_chain_intr(old_handler);
```

See Also

```
_dos_getvect, _dos_keep, _dos_setvect
```

__disable, __enable ◄

Purpose

Use the _*disable* and _*enable* functions to turn interrupts off and on with a CLI and an STI instruction, respectively.

Syntax

```
#include <dos.h>
void _disable(void);
void _enable(void);
```

Example Call

```
_disable(); /* Turn off interrupts -- CLI */
_enable();  /* Interrupts back on -- STI  */
```

► __dos__allocmem, __dos__freemem

Purpose

Use *__dos__allocmem* to call DOS function 48h to allocate memory in 16-byte chunks (called "paragraphs") from a pool maintained by DOS. Use the companion function *__dos__freemem* to release the memory by calling DOS function 49h when you no longer need it.

Syntax

```
#include <dos.h>
unsigned _dos_allocmem (unsigned npara, unsigned *segadd);
unsigned _dos_freemem (unsigned memadd);
unsigned npara;        Number of 16-byte paragraphs to be allocated
unsigned *segadd;      Pointer to location where segment address of
                       allocated memory is returned by __dos__allocmem
unsigned memadd;       Segment address of memory to be freed by __dos__
                       freemem
```

Example Call

```
_dos_allocmem(16, &block_allocated); /* Allocate 256 bytes */
_dos_freemem(block_allocated);       /* Free the block     */
```

Returns

Both functions return 0 if the operation is successful. Otherwise, the return value is the MS-DOS error code and the global variable *errno* is set to the constant ENOMEM.

See Also

```
calloc, _dos_setblock, free, halloc, malloc, realloc
```

► __dos__close

Purpose

Use *__dos__close* to call DOS function number 3Eh to close a file that you had opened earlier by calling *__dos__open* or that you had created by using *__dos__creat* or *__dos__creatnew*.

__dos__close

Syntax

```
#include <dos.h>
unsigned _dos_close (int filehandle);
int filehandle;        The file handle or identifier
```

Example Call

```
_dos_close(handle);
```

Returns

This function returns 0 if successful; otherwise, it returns the MS-DOS error code and sets the global variable *errno* to the constant EBADF indicating that the file handle is invalid.

See Also

```
close, _dos_creat, _dos_creatnew, _dos_open, open
```

__dos__creat, __dos__creatnew ◄

Purpose

Use *__dos__creat* to call the DOS function 3Ch to create a new file or to truncate an existing file to zero length. Use *__dos__creatnew* (DOS function 5Bh) when you don't want to overwrite an existing file.

The *attribute* argument is used to indicate whether a file is read-only, hidden, and so on. You can specify the attribute by using the bitwise OR of attribute names picked from Table 16-6. The attribute constants are defined in *dos.h*.

Table 16-6. Interpretation of File Attribute Constants

Attribute Name	Interpretation of This Attribute
_A_NORMAL	Normal file without any read or write restrictions.
_A_RDONLY	File cannot be opened for write operations.
_A_HIDDEN	File will not show up on directory search.
_A_SYSTEM	File is marked as a system file. It will be excluded from normal directory searches.
_A_VOLID	Volume name; can exist only in root directory.
_A_SUBDIR	Subdirectory name (means the file is a subdirectory).
_A_ARCH	If set, file will be archived by MS-DOS *BACKUP* command. This attribute is set after any changes to the file.

Syntax

```
#include <dos.h>
unsigned _dos_creat (char *filename, unsigned attribute,
                                     int *filehandle);
```

```
unsigned _dos_creatnew (char *filename, unsigned attribute,
                                        int *filehandle);
char    *filename;        File name, including path
unsigned attribute;       Attributes of the file
int     *filehandle;      Pointer to location where the "handle" or
                          identifier will be returned
```

Example Call

```
_dos_creat("c:\\tmp\\tmp001", _A_NORMAL, &filehandle);
_dos_creatnew("c:\\mceg\\ch16.1", _A_NORMAL, &filehandle);
```

Returns

Both functions return 0 if successful; otherwise, they return the MS-DOS error code and set the global variable *errno* to an error code.

See Also

```
close, creat, _dos_close, _dos_open, open
```

► __dos__findfirst, __dos__findnext

Purpose

Use *_dos_findfirst* to call DOS function 4Eh to find the first file whose name and attributes match the specified values. Since the specified name can have wildcard characters (* and ?), you can use this function to find, for example, the first file with a .*C* extension by searching for all *.*C* files. Once you find the first file, use *_dos_findnext* to call DOS function 4Fh to find the remaining instances of files whose names and attributes match the values used during the *_dos_findfirst* call. Use the constants shown in Table 16-6 to specify file attributes. The results of the search are returned in a *find _t* structure, which is declared in *dos.h* as shown in the following listing.

```
struct find_t
{
    char reserved[21];   /* Reserved for use by MS-DOS */
    char attrib;         /* Attribute byte of file     */
    unsigned wr_time;    /* Time of last file update   */
    unsigned wr_date;    /* Date of last file update   */
    long size;           /* File's length in bytes     */
    char name[13];       /* Null-terminated file name  */
};
```

Syntax

```
#include <dos.h>
void _dos_findfirst(char *filename, unsigned attribute,
                                    struct find_t *fileinfo);
```

__dos__findfirst, __dos__findnext

```
void _dos_findnext(struct find_t *fileinfo);
char *filename;              File name to search for including path
unsigned attribute;          File attributes to match
struct find_t *fileinfo;     Structure to hold results of search
```

Example Call

```
/* Search for all *.C files in current directory */
if (_dos_findfirst("*.c", _A_NORMAL, &fileinfo) != 0)
{
    printf("%s    %ld bytes\n", fileinfo.name,
                                fileinfo.size);
    while (_dos_findnext(&fileinfo) == 0)
        printf("%s    %ld bytes\n", fileinfo.name,
                                    fileinfo.size);
}
```

Returns

Both functions return 0 if successful; otherwise, they return the
MS-DOS error code and set *errno* to the constant ENOENT indicating that the file could not be found.

Example

Example 16-3 uses *_dos_findfirst* and *_dos_findnext* to list
all files with a .C extension.

__dos__getdate, __dos__setdate ◄

Purpose

Use *_dos_getdate* to call DOS function 2Ah to get the current
system date, as maintained by DOS. The *_dos_setdate* function
calls DOS function 2Bh to change the system date. The components of the date—the day, the month, the year, and the day of
the week—are stored in a *dosdate_t* structure, which is defined
in *dos.h* as:

```
struct dosdate_t
{
unsigned char day;      /* day of the month (range 1-31) */
unsigned char month;    /* month (range 1-12)            */
unsigned int year;      /* year (range 1980-2099)        */
unsigned char dayofweek;/* Day of the week 0-6, 0=Sunday */
};
```

Syntax

```
#include <dos.h>
void _dos_getdate (struct  dosdate_t *date);
unsigned _dos_setdate (struct  dosdate_t *date);
```

```
struct  dosdate_t *date;        Pointer to a structure that holds the
                                components of date
```

Example Call

```
_dos_getdate(&date);
_dos_setdate(&date);
```

See Also

```
_dos_gettime, _dos_settime, localtime, _strdate, _strtime
```

► **__dos__getdiskfree**

Purpose

Use *__dos__getdiskfree* to call the DOS function 36h to determine the total capacity of a disk, as well as the amount of free
space. The requested information is returned in a *diskfree_t*
structure whose address you provide in the argument *dfinfo*.
The data structure is declared in *dos.h* as:

```
struct diskfree_t
{
    unsigned total_clusters;
    unsigned avail_clusters;
    unsigned sectors_per_cluster;
    unsigned bytes_per_sector;
};
```

Syntax

```
#include <dos.h>
unsigned _dos_getdiskfree(unsigned drive, struct diskfree_t
                                                     *dfinfo);
unsigned drive;             Drive number, 0=default, 1=A, 2=B
struct diskfree_t *dfinfo;  Structure to hold information on disk
                            space
```

Example Call

```
_dos_getdiskfree (0, &dfinfo);
```

Returns

The function returns a zero if successful. It returns a nonzero
value in case of an error and sets the global variable *errno* to
EINVAL, indicating an invalid drive number.

See Also

```
_dos_getdrive, _dos_setdrive
```

__dos__getdiskfree

Example

Line 10 in Example 16-4 uses _dos_getdiskfree to find information about the total capacity and the available space on the current drive.

__dos__getdrive, __dos__setdrive ◄

Purpose

Use _dos_getdrive to call DOS function 19h to determine the
current default drive number while _dos_setdrive calls DOS
function 0Eh to change to a new default drive number.

Syntax

```
#include <dos.h>
void _dos_getdrive (unsigned *p_driveno);
void _dos_setdrive (unsigned driveno, unsigned *maxdrives);
```
unsigned *p_driveno;   *Pointer to location where current default drive*
                          number is to be returned by _ dos _ getdrive
                          (1=A, 2=B, and so on)
unsigned driveno;   *New default drive number for _ dos _ setdrive*
                          (1=A, 2=B, and so on)
unsigned *maxdrives;   *Pointer to location where _ dos _ setdrive*
                          returns the total number of logical drives

Example Call

```
_dos_getdrive(&drive_number);
_dos_setdrive(1, &maxdrives); /* New drive is A: */
```

Example

Line 9 in Example 16-4 uses _dos_getdrive to get the current
drive number.

__dos__getfileattr, __dos__setfileattr ◄

Purpose

Use _dos_getfileattr and _dos_setfileattr to call DOS function 43h to get and set the current attributes of a file, respectively. For example, you can use _dos_setfileattr to make a file
"hidden" so that it does not show up on an MS-DOS *DIR* command. See Table 16-6 for a list of file attributes.

Syntax

```
#include <dos.h>
```

```
void _dos_getfileattr(char *filename, unsigned *p_attribute);
void _dos_setfileattr(char *filename, unsigned attribute);
char *filename;                 File name, including path
unsigned *p_attribute;          Pointer to location where _dos_getfileattr
                                returns the attribute
unsigned attribute;             New file attribute for use by _dos_setfileattr
                                (Use constants from Table 16-6.)
```

Example Call

```
_dos_getfileattr("c:\\autoexec.bat", &attribute);
_setfileattr("secret.dat", _A_HIDDEN); /* Hide file */
```

Returns

Both functions return 0 if successful; otherwise, they return the MS-DOS error code and set the global variable *errno* to the constant ENOENT indicating that the file could not be found.

See Also

```
access, chmod
```

Example

Example 16-2 uses *_dos_setfileattr* in a program that hides a file or makes it visible again.

► **__dos__getftime, __dos__setftime**

Purpose

For each file, DOS records the time and date when the file was last modified. This information is maintained in coded form. The date is stored in a 16-bit word whose bits are interpreted as shown in Table 16-7.

Table 16-7. Codes That Show When File Last Modified

Bits	Contents
0–4	Day of the month (value between 1 and 31).
5–8	Month (value between 1 and 12).
9–15	Years since 1980 (e.g., 1988 is stored as 8).

The last update time of the file is also maintained in a 16-bit word as shown in Table 16-8.

Use *_dos_getftime* and *_dos_setftime*, respectively, to call DOS function 57h to get and set this information. You will need a handle returned by a function such as *_dos_open* or *_dos_creat*.

Table 16-8. Codes That Show Last Update Time

Bits	Contents
0–4	Number of 2-second increments (value between 0 and 29).
5–10	Minutes (value between 0 and 59).
11–15	Hours (value between 0 and 23).

Syntax

```
#include <dos.h>
unsigned _dos_getftime(int filehandle, unsigned *p_date,
                                       unsigned *p_time);
unsigned _dos_setftime(int filehandle, unsigned date,
                                       unsigned time);
```

int filehandle;	*The file handle or identifier*
unsigned *p_date;	*Pointer to location to hold date information*
unsigned *p_time;	*Pointer to location to hold time information*
unsigned date;	*Date information in packed form*
unsigned time;	*Time information in packed form*

Example Call

```
_dos_getftime(handle, &date, &time);
_dos_setftime(filehandle, date, time);
```

Returns

Both functions return 0 if successful; otherwise, they return the MS-DOS error code and set the global variable *errno* to the constant EBADF indicating that the file handle is invalid.

See Also

```
_dos_close, _dos_creat, _dos_creatnew, _dos_open, utime
```

__dos__gettime, __dos__settime ◄

Purpose

Use *_dos_gettime* to call DOS function 2Ch to get the current system time as maintained by DOS. You can use *_dos_settime* to call DOS function 2Dh to change the system time. The components of the time—the hour, the minutes, the seconds, and the hundredth of a second—are stored in fields of a *dostime_t* structure, which is defined in *dos.h* as:

```
struct dostime_t
{
    unsigned char hour;      /* Hour (range 0-23)      */
    unsigned char minute;    /* Minutes (range 0-59)   */
    unsigned char second;    /* Seconds (range 0-59)   */
    unsigned char hsecond;   /* Hundredth of a second*/
};
```

Syntax

```
#include <dos.h>
void _dos_gettime (struct  dostime_t *time);
void _dos_settime (struct  dostime_t *time);
struct  dostime_t *time;        Pointer to a structure that will hold the
                                components of time
```

Example Call

```
_dos_gettime(&time_info);
if(_dos_settime(&time_info) != 0)
               perror("Error setting time");
```

Returns

The *_dos_settime* function returns a zero if the operation is successful. Otherwise, it returns a nonzero value and sets the global variable *errno* to the constant *EINVAL*.

See Also

```
_dos_getdate, _dos_setdate, localtime, _strdate, _strtime
```

► __dos__getvect, __dos__setvect

Purpose

Use *_dos_getvect* to call DOS function 35h to get the current value of the interrupt vector for a specific interrupt number. The interrupt vector is the address of the routine that is invoked when the interrupt occurs. A new interrupt handler may be installed by using *_dos_setvect*, which calls DOS function 25h.

Syntax

```
#include <dos.h>
void (interrupt far *_dos_getvect (unsigned intno))();
void _dos_setvect (unsigned intno,
                    void(interrupt far *handler)());
unsigned intno;                 Interrupt number
interrupt far *handler;         Far pointer to the new handler, a function
                                of type interrupt
```

__dos__getvect, __dos__setvect

Example Call

```
void (interrupt far *int_handler)();
void interrupt far our_handler(void);
int_handler = _dos_getvect(int_number);
_dos_setvect(int_number, our_handler);
```

Returns

The _dos_getvect_ function returns a far pointer to the interrupt handler, which is a function of type *interrupt*. This is a keyword introduced in Microsoft C 5.0 to allow writing interrupt handlers in C. (See Chapter 1 for more details.)

See Also

_chain_intr, _dos_keep

__dos__keep ◄

Purpose

Use _dos_keep_ to call DOS function 31h to install the current program in memory, reserving the number of paragraphs specified in the argument *memsize*. Then it exits the program, returning the value specified in *status* to its parent (normally DOS). This is used to install "terminate-and-stay-resident" (TSR) programs.

Syntax

```
#include <dos.h>
void _dos_keep(unsigned status, unsigned memsize);
unsigned status;        Status code to be returned to calling process
unsigned memsize;       Size of memory needed by TSR program, in 16-byte
                        paragraphs
```

Example Call

```
_dos_keep(0, programsize_in_paragraphs);
```

See Also

_chain_intr, _dos_getvect, _dos_setvect

__dos__open ◄

Purpose

Use _dos_open_ to open an existing file by calling DOS function number 3Dh. The operations that can be performed on the file are indicated by the argument *mode*, which may be specified by the bitwise OR of one mode name from each category in Table 16-9.

Table 16-9. List of Modes in Which Files Can Be Opened

Category Name	Mode Name	Interpretation of the Mode
Access	O_RDONLY	Only reading allowed.
	O_WRONLY	Only writing allowed.
	O_RDWR	Both reading and writing allowed.
Sharing	SH_COMPAT	No other process can access the file.
	SH_DENYRW	No one else can read from or write to this file.
	SH_DENYWR	No one else can write to this file.
	SH_DENYRD	No one else can read from this file.
	SH_DENYNONE	File is completely shareable.
Inheritance	O_NOINHERIT	File will not be inherited by any child process.

Syntax

```
#include <dos.h>
#include <fcntl.h>        For permission names
#include <share.h>        For sharing modes
unsigned _dos_open (char *filename, unsigned mode,
                    int *filehandle);
char      *filename;      File name including path
unsigned  mode;           Permissions for operations to be performed on
                          the file
int       *filehandle;    Pointer to location where the file handle, or
                          identifier, will be returned
```

Example Call

```
_dos_open("dbindex.1", SH_COMPAT|O_RDONLY, &filehandle);
```

Returns

This function returns 0 if successful; otherwise, it returns the MS-DOS error code and sets the global variable *errno* to an error code.

See Also

```
close, _dos_close, _dos_creat, _dos_creatnew, open
```

__dos__open

__dos__read, __dos__write ◄

Purpose

Use __dos_read_ to read a specified number of bytes from a file into a buffer using DOS function 3Fh. You can write a buffer to a file by calling __dos_write_, which uses DOS function 40h. You will need a handle returned by a function such as __dos_open_ or __dos_creat_ before calling these functions.

Syntax

```
#include <dos.h>
unsigned _dos_read(int filehandle, void far *buffer,
                   unsigned count, unsigned *bytes_xfrd);
unsigned _dos_write(int filehandle, void far *buffer,
                unsigned count, unsigned *bytes_xfrd);
```

int filehandle;	*The file handle or identifier*
void far *buffer;	*Pointer to buffer for data transfer*
unsigned count;	*Number of bytes to be transferred*
unsigned *bytes_xfrd;	*Pointer to location that will contain the actual number of bytes transferred*

Example Call

```
_dos_read(filehandle, pbuf, 80, &bytes_read);
_dos_write(filehandle, pbuf, 80, &bytes_written);
```

Returns

Both functions return 0 if successful. Otherwise, they return the MS-DOS error code and set the global variable *errno* to an error code.

See Also

close, _dos_close, _dos_open, open, read, write

__dos__setblock ◄

Purpose

Use __dos_setblock_ to call DOS function 4Ah to adjust the size of a block of memory previously allocated by __dos_allocmem_.

Syntax

```
#include <dos.h>
unsigned _dos_setblock (unsigned newsize, unsigned segadd,
                        unsigned *maxavail);
```

```
unsigned newsize;        New size of block in units of 16-byte paragraphs
unsigned segadd;         Segment address of block
unsigned *maxavail;      Pointer to location that upon failure will be set to
                         the maximum number of paragraphs available
```

Example Call

```
_dos_setblock (16, segadd, &maxsize);
```

Returns

This function returns 0 if memory was successfully allocated. Otherwise, the return value is the MS-DOS error code, and the global variable *errno* is set to the constant ENOMEM.

See Also

```
calloc, _dos_allocmem, _dos_freemem, free, malloc, realloc
```

 **dosexterr**

Purpose

On MS-DOS 3.0 or later, use *dosexterr* to call DOS function 59h after an error return from a DOS function to obtain detailed information on the exact cause of the error and possible remedial action. The information about the error is returned in a DOSER-ROR structure, which is defined in *dos.h* as shown in the following listing.

```
struct DOSERROR
{
    int  exterror;   /* Extended error code */
    char class;      /* Error class         */
    char action;     /* Recommended action  */
    char locus;      /* Error locus -- device
                        where it occurred    */
};
```

For more detailed information on the fields of DOSERROR, consult the *Microsoft MS-DOS Programmer's Reference Manual* available from Microsoft Corporation.

Syntax

```
#include <dos.h>
int dosexterr (struct DOSERROR *errbuf);
struct DOSERROR *errbuf;    Pointer to structure that will contain
                            information on return
```

Example Call

```
dosexterr(&errbuf);
```

dosexterr

Returns

The return value is identical to the field *exterror*, which is the value of the *AX* register.

See Also

perror, _strerror, strerror

FP_OFF, FP_SEG ◀

Purpose

Use the *FP_OFF* and *FP_SEG* macros to get the "segment" address and the "offset" of a far pointer, respectively.

Syntax

```
#include <dos.h>
unsigned FP_OFF(char far *address);
unsigned FP_SEG(char far *address);
char far *address;     Far pointer to memory location
```

Example Call

```
offset_buf = FP_OFF(p_buf); /* p_buf is a far pointer */
segadd_buf = FP_SEG(p_buf);
```

Returns

FP_OFF returns the offset, and *FP_SEG* returns the segment address of the far pointer *address*.

See Also

segread

__harderr, __hardresume, __hardretn ◀

Purpose

Use *_harderr* to install a new handler for interrupt number 24h (critical error) that will call the routine whose address you provide in the argument *funcptr*. This interrupt occurs on hardware errors during I/O operations such as trying to read from a diskette with the drive door open. The *_hardresume* and *_hardretn* functions are used in the INT 24h handler to exit to DOS or return to the application, respectively. The argument *returncode* tells error handler what to do upon returning to DOS. Use one of the predefined constants given in Table 16-10 to specify the action. These constants are defined in *dos.h*. Consult *The Waite Group's Microsoft C Bible* for further details on writing a critical error handler in Microsoft C.

Table 16-10. Error Codes Accepted by _ *hardresume*

Return Code Constant	Action Taken by MS-DOS
_ HARDERR _ IGNORE	Ignore the error.
_ HARDERR _ RETRY	Retry the operation that caused the error.
_ HARDERR _ ABORT	Abort the program by invoking INT 23h.
_ HARDERR _ FAIL	Fail the MS-DOS system call in progress (only under MS-DOS 3.0 and later).

Syntax

```
#include <dos.h>
void _harderr (void (far *funcptr)());
void _hardresume (int returncode);
void _hardretn (int errorcode);
void (far *funcptr)();        Far pointer to the function that will be called
                              by the new INT 24h handler
int returncode;               Tells DOS how the handler is returning
int errorcode;                MS-DOS error code returned to application
                              program
```

Example Call

```
void far harderror_handler(unsigned, unsigned,
                            unsigned far *);
_harderr(harderror_handler);
_hardresume(_HARDERR_ABORT);  /* Abort program */
_hardretn(-1);                /* Return to DOS */
```

See Also

_chain_intr, _dos_getvect, _dos_keep, _dos_setvect

► int86, int86x

Purpose

Use the *int86* and *int86x* functions to invoke any BIOS and DOS service routines that can be accessed by generating an 8086 software interrupt. You should use *int86x* when the function called by the interrupt requires arguments placed in the segment registers *DS* and *ES*. Otherwise, the *int86* function is sufficient. The functions use the *union* REGS and *struct* SREGS to pass register values back and forth. These data structures are defined in *dos.h* as:

```
struct WORDREGS
{
    unsigned int ax, bx, cx, dx, si, di, cflag;
};
struct BYTEREGS
{
    unsigned char al, ah, bl, bh, cl, ch, dl, dh;
};
union REGS
{
    struct WORDREGS x;
    struct BYTEREGS h;
};
struct SREGS
{
    unsigned int es, cs, ss, ds;
};
```

Syntax

```
#include <dos.h>
int int86(int intno, union REGS *inregs, union REGS *outregs);
int int86x(int intno, union REGS *inregs,
           union REGS *outregs, struct SREGS *segregs);
```
int	intno;	*Interrupt number*
union	REGS * inregs;	*Input registers*
union	REGS * outregs;	*Output registers*
struct	SREGS * segregs;	*Segment registers*

Example Call

```
union REGS   inregs, outregs;
struct SREGS segregs;
int86(0x10, &inregs, &outregs);
int86x(0x21, &inregs, &outregs, &segregs);
```

Returns

Each function returns the contents of the AX register after the interrupt. Error is indicated by a nonzero value in *outregs.x.cflag*.

See Also

bdos, intdos, intdosx

---

intdos, intdosx ◀

Purpose

Use *intdos* and *intdosx* to access the MS-DOS functions. You should use *intdosx* when the DOS function requires you to exchange arguments through the segment registers *DS* and *ES*. See *int86* for a description of the data structures REGS and SREGS.

Syntax

```
#include <dos.h>
int intdos( union REGS *inregs, union REGS *outregs)
int intdosx( union REGS *inregs, union REGS *outregs,
          struct SREGS *segregs);
union REGS    *inregs;      Input registers
union REGS    *outregs;     Output registers
struct SREGS  *segregs;     Segment registers
```

Example Call

```
union REGS xr, yr;
intdos(&inregs, &outregs);
```

Returns

Each function returns the value of the register *AX* after the interrupt. Error is indicated by a nonzero value in the field *outregs.x.cflag*.

See Also

```
bdos, bdosptr, geninterrupt, int86, int86x, intr
```

▶ segread

Purpose

Use the *segread* function to retrieve the values of the 80x86 segment registers *CS*, *DS*, *ES*, and *SS* from C programs. See *int86x* for the declaration of the SREGS structure.

Syntax

```
#include <dos.h>
void segread (struct SREGS *segregs);
struct SREGS *segregs;      SREGS structure to hold segment registers
```

Example Call

```
segread(&segregs);
```

See Also

```
int86x, intdosx
```

Example 16-1   Use *_bios_serialcom* to set up the serial port at 300 baud, 8-bit word length, 1 stop bit, and no parity. If you have a Hayes-compatible modem connected, once you have set the port,

segread

you can try conversing with it. For example, if
you enter AT, the modem should answer back
with an OK. (If there is no response, try entering ATE1V1 to set up the modem properly.)
This program assumes that you are using the
COM1 port.

```
1:#include <stdio.h>
2:#include <bios.h>
3:#define COM1 0    /* Change to 1 for COM2 */
4:main()
5:{
6:    int c;
7:    unsigned service, data, status;
8:    data = (_COM_CHR8 | _COM_STOP1 |_COM_NOPARITY |
9:          _COM_300);
10:   _bios_serialcom(_COM_INIT, COM1, data);
11:   printf("Connecting to serial port 1. "
12:          "Type 'q' to exit\n");
13:
14:   while(1)
15:   {
16:/* First see if "DATA READY" flag is set. If yes read
17: * character from serial port.
18: */
19:       status = 0x100 &
20:               _bios_serialcom(_COM_STATUS, COM1, 0);
21:       if (status == 0x100)
22:       {
23:/* If there is a character, get it and display it */
24:           c = 0xff &
25:               _bios_serialcom(_COM_RECEIVE, COM1, 0);
26:           printf("%c", c);
27:       }
28:
29:/* Now check if any key has been pressed */
30:       if(_bios_keybrd(_KEYBRD_READY))
31:       {
32:/* If yes, read the keyboard buffer */
33:           c = _bios_keybrd(_KEYBRD_READ) & 0xff;
34:           if((c == 'q') || (c == 'Q'))
35:           {
36:/* Exit if it's a 'q' or a 'Q' */
37:               printf("Exiting...\n");
38:               exit(0);
39:           }
40:
41:/* Else, wait until "transmit holding register empty"
42: * flag is set. Once it's set, send out character to
43: * serial port.
44: */
45:           status = 0x2000 &
46:               _bios_serialcom(_COM_STATUS, COM1, 0);
```

```
47:              while (status != 0x2000)
48:              {
49:                  status = 0x2000 &
50:                  _bios_serialcom(_COM_STATUS, COM1, 0);
51:              }
52:              _bios_serialcom(_COM_SEND, COM1, c);
53:              if ((status & 0x8000) == 0x8000)
54:              {
55:                  printf("Error sending: %c\n", c);
56:              }
57:          }
58:      }
59:}
```

Example 16-2   Use *_dos_fileattr* to write a utility program
                     capable of hiding a file or making it visible
                     again. The DIR command in MS-DOS will not
                     list files that are marked hidden.

```
 1:#include <stdio.h>
 2:#include <dos.h>
 3:
 4:#define UNHIDE  _A_NORMAL
 5:#define HIDE _A_HIDDEN
 6:#define H_MSG  "hidden"
 7:#define U_MSG  "visible"
 8:
 9:main(int argc, char **argv)
10:{
11:    int attr = 0;
12:    char *message;
13:    if(argc < 3)
14:    {
15:     printf("Usage %s <filename> <H|U>\n", argv[0]);
16:        exit(0);
17:    }
18:    if (argv[2][0] == 'H')
19:    {
20:        attr = HIDE;
21:        message = H_MSG;
22:    }
23:    else
24:    {
25:        if (argv[2][0] == 'U')
26:        {
27:            attr = UNHIDE;
28:            message = U_MSG;
29:        }
30:        else
31:        {
32:            printf("Unknown option: %s\n", argv[2]);
33:            exit(1);
34:        }
```

```
35:    }
36:/* Call _dos_setfileattr to set the attribute */
37:    if (_dos_setfileattr(argv[1], attr) != 0)
38:    {
39:        printf("Error in _dos_setfileattr call!\n");
40:        exit(0);
41:    }
42:    printf("%s is now %s. Try DIR to verify.\n",
43:        argv[1], message);
44:}
```

Example 16-3   Use *_dos_findfirst* and *_dos_findnext* to
find all files with a .C extension. You need to
call *_dos_findfirst* to set up the search and
get the first file that matches the specified
name and attribute.

```
1:#include <stdio.h>
2:#include <dos.h>
3:main()
4:{
5:    int count;
6:    long totalsize;
7:    struct find_t fileinfo;
8:    if (_dos_findfirst("*.c", _A_NORMAL, &fileinfo) != 0)
9:    {
10:        printf("Unsuccessful _dos_findfirst call!\n");
11:        exit(0);
12:    }
13:    printf("Listing of *.c files:\n");
14:    printf("%12s  %8ld bytes\n", fileinfo.name,
15:                                 fileinfo.size);
16:    count = 1;
17:    totalsize = fileinfo.size;
18:    while (_dos_findnext(&fileinfo) == 0)
19:    {
20:        count++;
21:        totalsize += fileinfo.size;
22:/* Now print the name and size of each matching file */
23:        printf("%12s  %8ld bytes\n",
24:                fileinfo.name, fileinfo.size);
25:    }
26:    printf("\n%d files %ld bytes.\n", count, totalsize);
27:}
```

Example 16-4   This program displays the total capacity of
your drive in bytes and the amount not in use.

```
1:#include <stdio.h>
2:#include <dos.h>
3:main()
4:{
5:    unsigned long total_space, free_space,
6:                    bytes_per_cluster;
```

```
7:     int drive;
8:     struct diskfree_t dfinfo;
9:     _dos_getdrive(&drive); /* Get current drive */
10:    if(_dos_getdiskfree(0, &dfinfo) != 0)
11:    {
12:        printf("Error in _dos_getdiskfree\n");
13:        exit(0);
14:    }
15:    bytes_per_cluster = dfinfo.sectors_per_cluster *
16:                        dfinfo.bytes_per_sector;
17:    total_space = dfinfo.total_clusters *
18:                  bytes_per_cluster;
19:    free_space = dfinfo.avail_clusters *
20:                 bytes_per_cluster;
21:    printf ("On drive %c:\n", drive+'A'-1);
22:    printf ("%ld bytes free out of %ld bytes of total "
23:            "space.\n", free_space, total_space);
24:}
```

V

Microsoft C Graphics

17

Graphics Modes, Coordinates, and Attributes

Increasingly, graphics user interfaces are the norm for PC-based applications, as the older text-based DOS makes way for OS/2 with its promise of a bit-mapped, window-oriented interface. Creating an effective screen-oriented program is difficult because of the variety of graphics adapters and displays that are used in PCs. Adding to this complexity is the IBM PC's limited support for video I/O in the ROM BIOS. (See Chapter 16.) All this changed with Microsoft C 5.0—thanks to the addition of over 40 graphics routines that make the task of creating graphics-based programs much simpler by providing the basic tools to anyone who programs in Microsoft C. The Microsoft C graphics routines are designed to perform well, and they provide all basic capabilities necessary to develop graphics applications. For example, there are routines to determine what video equipment is installed and set an appropriate video mode. You can select colors, line styles, and fill patterns; draw primitive shapes such as a straight line, rectangle, arc, and ellipse; mix text and graphics on the screen; and even perform animation by saving and restoring screen images.

In the next three chapters, we describe the graphics library routines that you will find in Microsoft C 5.1. This chapter presents the routines that control the graphics modes and attributes. Chapter 18 summarizes the drawing and animation routines, and Chapter 19, the routines for text output in graphics mode.

▶ __displaycursor

Purpose

Use *__displaycursor* to turn the solid cursor on or off while in the graphics mode. You can use the constants _GCURSORON and _GCURSOROFF to specify that the cursor be turned on and off, respectively.

Syntax

```
#include <graph.h>
short far _displaycursor(short on_off);
short on_off;     Selected display mode of cursor
```

Example Call

```
_displaycursor(_GCURSORON); /* Turn the block cursor on */
```

Returns

The return value is the previous value of the cursor state.

▶ __getbkcolor, __setbkcolor

Purpose

Use the *__getbkcolor* and *__setbkcolor* functions to get and set the value of the background color, respectively. The current video mode determines how you interpret and specify the background color. In text modes, the background color is a color number from the current palette. In graphics modes, you have to specify a long integer containing an RGB (Red-Green-Blue) value that is used by *__setbkcolor* to redefine the color number 0 in the current palette. You can use the color constants shown in Table 17-1 to specify the color.

Table 17-1. List of Color Names and Their RGB Values

Color Constant	Hexadecimal RGB Value
_BLACK	0x000000L
_BLUE	0x2a0000L
_GREEN	0x002a00L
_CYAN	0x2a2a00L
_RED	0x00002aL
_MAGENTA	0x2a002aL
_BROWN	0x00152aL
_WHITE	0x2a2a2aL
_GRAY	0x151515L

Table 17-1. (cont.)

Color Constant	Hexadecimal RGB Value
_LIGHTBLUE	0x3F1515L
_LIGHTGREEN	0x153f15L
_LIGHTCYAN	0x3f3f15L
_LIGHTRED	0x15153fL
_LIGHTMAGENTA	0x3f153fL
_LIGHTYELLOW	0x153f3fL
_BRIGHTWHITE	0x3f3f3fL

Syntax

```
#include <graph.h>
long far _getbkcolor(void);
long far _setbkcolor(long color);
long color;     New color value for __setbkcolor
```

Example Call

```
bcolor = _getbkcolor(); /* Retrieve background color */
_setbkcolor(4L);   /* Red background in text mode     */
_setbkcolor(_RED); /* Red background in graphics mode */
```

Returns

The _getbkcolor function returns the current background color while _setbkcolor returns the previous value.

See Also

```
_remapallpalette, _remappalette, _selectpalette
```

__getcolor, __setcolor ◄

Purpose

Use the _getcolor function to obtain the current color number. The current color may be set by calling _setcolor.

Syntax

```
#include <graph.h>
short far _getcolor(void);
short far _setcolor(short color);
short color;     Color number for __setcolor
```

Example Call

```
current_color = _getcolor();
_setcolor(4); /* Use color number 4, normally Red */
```

Returns

The *_getcolor* function returns the current color number, while *_setcolor* returns the previous value.

► _getfillmask, _setfillmask

Purpose

Use *_getfillmask* to retrieve the 8 bytes that define the 8x8 mask used by the routines *_floodfill*, *_rectangle*, *_ellipse*, and *_pie* that fill an area with the current color. Use *_setfillmask* to define a new fill pattern specified by the argument *fillmask*, which is a far pointer to an array of eight characters. Since each character has 8 bits, you can think of this 8 by 8 array of bits as a model of an area on the screen, 8 pixels wide and 8 pixels tall, with the first character representing the first row of the area. When filling an 8x8 area using the mask, those pixels that correspond to 0 bits are left untouched while the rest are filled with the current color. For areas larger than 8x8 pixels, the fill operation is done by repeatedly using the mask on successive 8x8 blocks of the screen until the entire area is covered. Thus, a solid fill is specified when all eight characters contain the value FFh. This is the default value of the fill style in the graphics package. Figure 17-1 illustrates the way the fill mask is used.

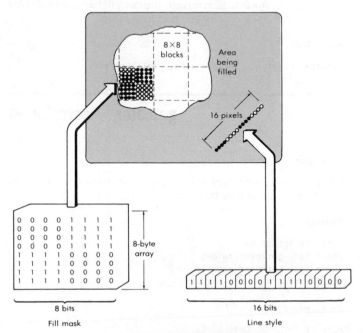

Figure 17-1. Fill mask and line style

Syntax

```
#include <graph.h>
unsigned char far * far _getfillmask(unsigned
                                    char far *fillmask);
void far _setfillmask(unsigned char far *fillmask);
unsigned char far *fillmask;    8x8 bit pattern that determines how
                                the filled area looks
```

Example Call

```
unsigned char far oldmask[8];
unsigned char far mask1[] =
          {1, 3, 7, 0xf, 0x1f, 0x3f, 0x7f, 0xff};
_getfillmask(old_mask);
_setfillmask(mask1);
```

Returns

If no mask is present, *_getfillmask* returns a NULL.

See Also

```
_getlinestyle, _setlinestyle
```

__getlinestyle, __setlinestyle ◄

Purpose

Use *_getlinestyle* to retrieve the 16-bit mask used by the routines *_lineto* and *_rectangle* when drawing straight lines. The mask controls how the line looks, and it can be set by calling *_setlinestyle*. The 16-bit argument *linemask* is used to specify the pattern to be repeated when drawing a line. Think of this mask as one representing a line segment 16 pixels long. If a bit in *linemask* is a 1, the corresponding pixel in that line gets painted with the current color (see *_setcolor*). If a bit is 0, the corresponding pixel is left untouched. Note that a value of FFFFh for *linemask* means a solid line. This is the default value of the line style in the graphics package. Figure 17-1 illustrates the way the line style is used.

Syntax

```
#include <graph.h>
unsigned short far _getlinestyle(void);
void far _setlinestyle(unsigned short linemask);
unsigned short linemask;    Bit pattern that determines how the line
                            looks (for _setlinestyle)
```

Example Call

```
line_style = _getlinestyle();
_setlinestyle(0x3ff);  /* Long dashes */
```

Returns

The *_getlinestyle* function returns the current line style.

See Also

```
_getfillmask, _setfillmask
```

Example

Example 17-1 shows a number of available line styles using *_set-linestyle*.

► __getlogcoord, __getphyscoord

Purpose

Use *_getlogcoord* to convert from physical coordinates to the logical ones and *_getphyscoord* to revert back.

Syntax

```
#include <graph.h>
struct xycoord far _getlogcoord(short x, short y);
struct xycoord far _getphyscoord(short x, short y);
short x, y;        The x and y coordinates of the point (physical for
                   _getlogcoord and logical for _getphyscoord)
```

Example Call

```
struct xycoord xy_logical, xy_physical;
xy_logical = _getlogcoord(x_physical, y_physical);
xy_physical = _getphyscoord(x_logical, y_logical);
```

Returns

Each function returns the appropriately converted coordinates of the specified pixel in a structure of type *xycoord*, which is declared in the header file *graph.h* as shown below:

```
struct xycoord          /* Structure for pixel coordinates */
{
    short xcoord;       /* x-coordinate */
    short ycoord;       /* y-coordinate */
};
```

See Also

```
_setlogorg
```

__getlogcoord, __getphyscoord

___getvideoconfig ◀

Purpose

Use ___getvideoconfig_ to obtain information about the current graphics environment. Values of parameters such as the maximum number of pixels along x and y directions, the number of colors, and more, are returned in a structure of type *videoconfig* defined in the file *graph.h* as shown below:

```
struct videoconfig {
    short numxpixels;    /*number of pixels along X axis       */
    short numypixels;    /*number of pixels along Y axis       */
    short numtextcols;   /*number of text columns available    */
    short numtextrows;   /*number of text rows available       */
    short numcolors;     /*number of actual colors             */
    short bitsperpixel;  /*number of bits per pixel            */
    short numvideopages; /*number of available video pages     */
    short mode;          /*current video mode                  */
    short adapter;       /*active display adapter              */
    short monitor;       /*active display monitor              */
    short memory;        /*adapter video memory in K bytes     */
};
```

The meaning of most of the fields in the structure is obvious from the comments in the declaration of the structure. The value of the fields *adapter*, *monitor*, and *mode* can be intrepreted by comparing each with the mnemonic constants shown in Tables 17-2, 17-3, and 17-4, respectively.

Table 17-2. Intrepreting Adapter Value

Adapter Name	Interpretation of the Name
_ MDPA	Monochrome Display Adapter
_ HGC	Hercules Graphics Card
_ CGA	Color Graphics Adapter
_ EGA	Enhanced Graphics Adapter
_ MCGA	MultiColor Graphics Array
_ VGA	Video Graphics Array

Table 17-3. Intrepreting Monitor Value

Monitor Name	Interpretation of the Name
_ MONO	Monochrome Monitor
_ COLOR	Color Monitor (or Enhanced monitor in CGA mode)
_ ENHCOLOR	Enhanced Color Monitor
_ ANALOG	Analog Monitor

Table 17-4. Microsoft C Graphics Modes

Mode Name	Interpretation of the Mode Name
_ DEFAULTMODE	Mode in which program first started
_ TEXTBW40	40 x 25 text in 16 shades of grey
_ TEXTC40	40 x 25 text in 16 or 8 colors
_ TEXTBW80	80 x 25 text in 16 shades of grey
_ TEXTC80	80 x 25 text in 16 or 8 color
_ MRES4COLOR	320 x 200 graphics in 4 color
_ MRESNOCOLOR	320 x 200 graphics in 4 shades of grey
_ HRESBW	640 x 200 graphics in black and white
_ TEXTMONO	80 x 25 text in black and white
_ HERCMONO	720 x 348, BW for Hercules Graphics Card
_ MRES16COLOR	320 x 200 graphics in 16 colors
_ HRES16COLOR	640 x 200 graphics in 16 colors
_ ERESNOCOLOR	640 x 350 graphics in black and white
_ ERESCOLOR	640 x 350 graphics in 4 or 16 colors
_ VRES2COLOR	640 x 480 graphics in black and white
_ VRES16COLOR	640 x 480 graphics in 16 colors
_ MRES256COLOR	320 x 200 graphics in 256 colors

Syntax

```
#include <graph.h>
struct videoconfig far * far _getvideoconfig(struct
                              videoconfig far *gr_info);
struct videoconfig far *gr_info;        Pointer to structure that will
                                        hold the information about the
                                        graphics environment
```

Example Call

```
_getvideoconfig(&gr_info);
```

Returns

The *_getvideoconfig* function returns the pointer that you had supplied in the argument *gr_info*.

See Also

```
_setvideomode
```

Example

Example 17-1 shows how *_getvideoconfig* can be used to determine the graphics hardware and select a suitable graphics mode.

__getvideoconfig

__remapallpalette, __remappalette ◀

Purpose

Use *__remapallpalette* in an EGA or VGA environment to redefine how the values that a pixel can take are associated with colors displayed on the screen. Thus, this function redefines the entire EGA or VGA palette. The *__remappalette* function, on the other hand, redefines a single pixel value in EGA or VGA palette.

Syntax

```
#include <graph.h>
short far _remapallpalette(long far *color_array);
long far _remappalette(short pixel_value, long color);
```

`long far *color_array;`	*Array of colors that will be assigned sequentially to the pixel values (Use predefined constants from Table 17-1.)*
`short pixel_value;`	*Pixel value to be redefined by __remappalette*
`long color;`	*Color __remappalette associates with the pixel value (Use predefined constants from Table 17-1.)*

Example Call

```
_remapallpalette(&new_color_table);
_remappalette(0, _CYAN);/* Alter pixel value 0 to cyan */
```

Returns

If the hardware is EGA or VGA, the *__remapallpalette* function returns a 0 and the *remappalette* function returns a long integer containing the previous color associated with the pixel value that has been redefined. If the hardware is of the wrong type, both functions return −1, indicating an error.

See Also

```
_setbkcolor, _setcolor
```

__selectpalette ◀

Purpose

Use the *__selectpalette* function to activate one of up to four predefined palettes when using the CGA or the EGA in "__MRES4COLOR" and "__MRESNOCOLOR" video modes.

Syntax

```
#include <graph.h>
short far _selectpalette(short palette_number);
short palette_number;      Palette number being selected
```

Example Call

```
_selectpalette(0);      /* Select CGA palette 0 */
```

Returns

The *_selectpalette* function returns the previous palette number.

See Also

```
_getvideoconfig, _setvideomode
```

► __setactivepage, __setvisualpage

Purpose

Use the *_setactivepage* function in EGA or VGA graphics modes and in the text modes to select the current "page" or portion of display memory where graphics and text operations are performed. This function will work only when the adapter has enough video memory to support multiple pages. The *_setvisualpage* function is for selecting the video page to be displayed.

Syntax

```
#include <graph.h>
short far _setactivepage(short page_number);
short far _setvisualpage(short page_number);
short page_number;      The page number to be used
```

Example Call

```
_setactivepage(0);  /* Draw in page 0 while       */
_setactivepage(1);  /* page 1 is being displayed */
```

Returns

Both functions return the previous page number. In case of error, the return value is negative.

See Also

```
_getvideoconfig
```

__setactivepage, __setvisualpage

__setcliprgn, __setviewport ◀

Purpose

Use _setcliprgn_ to define a rectangular region of the screen as the clipping region for graphics (i.e., any graphics falling outside this region will be cut off). The _setviewport_ behaves similarly, but it also sets the origin of the logical coordinate system at the upper-left corner of the clipping region (this is known as a "viewport").

Syntax

```
#include <graph.h>
void far _setcliprgn(short x1, short y1, short x2, short y2);
void far _setviewport(short x1, short y1, short x2, short y2);
short x1, y1;    Upper-left corner of clipping region in physical
                 coordinates
short x2, y2;    Lower-right corner of clipping region in physical
                 coordinates
```

Example Call

```
_setcliprgn(100, 50, 300, 150);
_setviewport(150, 50, 350, 150);
```

See Also

```
_setlogorg, _settexttextwindow, _setviewport
```

__setlogorg ◀

Purpose

Use _setlogorg_ to move the origin (the point 0,0) of the logical coordinate system used for graphics to a specific physical pixel location on the display screen. The physical coordinates are with respect to a coordinate frame whose origin is fixed to the upper-left corner of the screen, while the logical coordinate system can be moved about by using _setlogorg_. All drawing functions in Chapter 18 use logical coordinates.

Syntax

```
#include <graph.h>
struct xycoord far _setlogorg(short x, short y);
short x, y;    The physical x and y coordinates of the point on the screen
               that becomes the new origin of the logical coordinate
               system
```

Example Call

```
_setlogorg(100, 100);
```

Returns

The *_setlogorg* function returns the coordinates of the previous logical origin in a structure of type *xycoord* (see *_getlogcoord*).

See Also

```
_getlogcoord, _getphyscoord, _setviewport
```

► __setvideomode

Purpose

Use *_setvideomode* to set a display mode appropriate for a particular combination of adapter (video card) and display (monitor). Table 17-4 shows the mode names defined in *graph.h*.

Syntax

```
#include <graph.h>
short far _setvideomode(short mode);
short mode;        Selected mode (Use constant from Table 17-4.)
```

Example Call

```
_setvideomode(_ERESCOLOR); /* 640 x 350 in 4 or 16 colors */
```

Returns

The return value is nonzero if everything goes well. If the specified mode is not supported by the hardware configuration, then *_setvideomode* will return a zero.

See Also

```
_getvideoconfig
```

Example

Example 17-1 shows how *_setvideomode* is used to enable a graphics mode.

Example 17-1   This example uses *_getvideoconfig* to determine the current display adapter and monitor present on the PC and to select an appropriate graphics mode. Then it enters the graphics mode and displays a number of possible line styles.

```
1:#include <stdio.h>
2:#include <stdio.h>
```

__setvideomode

```
 3:#include <conio.h>
 4:#include <graph.h>
 5:
 6:/* Define the line style masks */
 7:short linemask[16] =
 8:{1, 3, 7, 0xf, 0x1f, 0x3f, 0x7f, 0xff, 0x1ff,
 9: 0x3ff, 0x7ff, 0xfff, 0x1fff, 0x3fff, 0x7fff, 0xffff};
10:
11:main()
12:{
13:    struct videoconfig gr_info, far *p_gr;
14:    short videomode = _DEFAULTMODE, i, y=30;
15:/* Get the current video configuration. */
16:    p_gr = _getvideoconfig(&gr_info);
17:    printf("This PC has:\n");
18:/* You can access the structure using the returned
19: * pointer
20: */
21:    switch(p_gr->adapter)   /* Select a video mode */
22:    {
23:      case _MDPA: printf("Monochrome Display Adapter");
24:                  break;
25:      case _HGC: printf("Hercules Graphics Card");
26:                  videomode = _HERCMONO;
27:                  break;
28:      case _CGA: printf("Color Graphics Adapter");
29:                  videomode = _HRESBW;
30:                  break;
31:      case _EGA: printf("Enhanced Graphics Adapter");
32:                  videomode = _ERESCOLOR;
33:                  break;
34:      case _MCGA: printf("Multicolor Graphics Array");
35:                  videomode = _VRES2COLOR;
36:                  break;
37:      case _VGA: printf("Video Graphics Array");
38:                  videomode = _VRES16COLOR;
39:                  break;
40:    }
41:    printf(" and ");
42:/* Or, you can access the structure directly */
43:    switch(gr_info.monitor)
44:    {
45:      case _MONO:     printf("Monochrome Monitor\n");
46:                  break;
47:      case _COLOR:    printf("Color Monitor "
48:                  "(or Enhanced monitor in CGA mode)\n");
49:                  break;
50:      case _ENHCOLOR: printf("Enhanced Color Monitor\n");
51:                  break;
52:      case _ANALOG:   printf("Analog Monitor\n");
53:                  break;
54:    }
```

```
55:    if(videomode == _DEFAULTMODE) exit(0);
56:    printf("\nPress any key to see line styles...");
57:    getch();
58:/* Set video mode */
59:    if (_setvideomode(videomode) == 0)
60:    {
61:/* Error setting mode */
62:        printf("\nError setting mode. Exiting...\n");
63:        exit(1);
64:    }
65:    _settextposition(1,1);
66:    _outtext("Demonstrating different line styles:");
67:    for (i=0; i<16; i++)
68:    {
69:/* Select a line style from the array of style masks */
70:        _setlinestyle(linemask[i]);
71:        _moveto(0,y);
72:        _lineto(500,y);
73:        y += 10;
74:    }
75:/* Restore original mode */
76:/* Give user a chance to see the result */
77:    _settextposition(40,1);
78:    _outtext("Press any key to exit:");
79:    getch();
80:    _setvideomode(_DEFAULTMODE);
81:}
```

18

Drawing and Animation

The Microsoft C graphics library includes a set of routines to draw basic shapes and manipulate color bit-mapped images. The library currently has provisions for drawing arcs, ellipses, pie slices, and rectangles. Many of these figures can be optionally filled with the current fill color using the current fill pattern (described in Chapter 17). The image manipulation routines are capable of saving a rectangular area of the screen in a buffer and restoring the image from the buffer at a specified screen coordinate. These functions can be used to achieve "animation," which is the process of creating the visual effect of motion of an object on the screen. The drawing routines are the building blocks for your graphics applications. With the basic shapes and the ability to color pixels at arbitrary screen coordinates, you can draw quite complicated images on the screen. This chapter summarizes the 14 drawing and image manipulation routines available in the Microsoft C graphics library.

► _arc

Purpose

Use *_arc* to draw a segment of an ellipse using the current color. Figure 18-1 illustrates the interpretation of the arguments to *arc*.

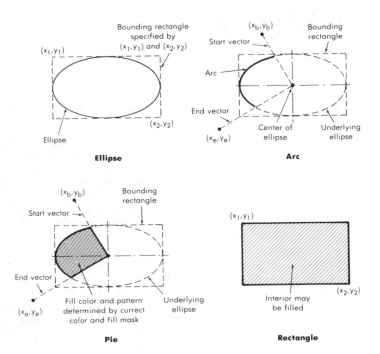

Figure. 18-1. Specifications for ellipse, arc, pie, and rectangle

Syntax

```
#include <graph.h>
short far _arc(short x1, short y1, short x2, short y2,
               short xb, short yb, short xe, short ye);
```

short x1, y1;	*Coordinates of upper-left corner of bounding rectangle of the ellipse to which the arc belongs*
short x2, y2;	*Coordinates of lower-right corner of bounding rectangle of the ellipse to which the arc belongs*
short xb, yb;	*The arc begins at the point where a line drawn from the center of the bounding rectangle to (xb, yb) cuts the ellipse*
short xe, ye;	*The arc ends at the point where a line drawn from the center of the bounding rectangle to (xe, ye) cuts the ellipse*

Example Call

```
_arc(100, 50, 250, 100, 0, 50, 250, 100);
```

Returns

The *_arc* function returns a nonzero value if all goes well. Otherwise, it returns zero.

See Also

```
_setcolor
```

__clearscreen ◄

Purpose

Use *_clearscreen* to clear an area of the screen and fill it with the current background color. The area to be cleared is indicated by the parameter *area*, which should be set to one of the constants shown in Table 18-1.

Table 18-1. Interpreting Area Constants

Constant	Interpretation
_GCLEARSCREEN	Entire screen is cleared and filled.
_GVIEWPORT	Only current viewport is cleared and filled. (See *_setviewport*.)
_GWINDOW	Only current text window is cleared and filled. (See *_settextwindow*.)

Syntax

```
#include <graph.h>
void far _clearscreen(short area);
short area;      Constant indicating area to be cleared
```

Example Call

```
_clearscreen(_GCLEARSCREEN); /* Clear the entire screen */
```

See Also

```
_setbkcolor, _settextwindow, _setviewport
```

__ellipse ◄

Purpose

Use *_ellipse* to draw a filled or a bordered ellipse that you specify by the corners of the bounding rectangle. The argument *flag* controls whether the ellipse is filled or not. Table 18-2 shows the possible values of *flag*.

Table 18-2. Interpreting the Fill Flag

Fill Flag	Interpretation of the Constant
_GFILLINTERIOR	Fills the figure using the current color (see _setcolor) and the current fill mask (see _setfillmask).
_GBORDER	Only the outline of the figure is drawn.

Syntax

```
#include <graph.h>
short far _ellipse(short flag, short x1, short y1,
                                short x2, short y2);
short flag;          To fill or to draw a border
short x1, y1;        Coordinates of upper-left corner of rectangle
                     circumscribing the ellipse
short x2, y2;        Coordinates of lower-right corner rectangle
                     circumscribing the ellipse
```

Example Call

```
_ellipse(_GFILLINTERIOR, 100, 100, 200, 300);
```

Returns

The return value is nonzero if everything went well. Otherwise, *_ellipse* returns a zero.

See Also

```
_floodfill, _setcolor, _setfillmask
```

► __floodfill

Purpose

Use the *_floodfill* function to fill an area of the screen with the current color (see *_setcolor*) and using the current fill mask (see *_setfillmask*).

Syntax

```
#include <graph.h>
short far _floodfill(short x, short y, short boundary_color);
short x, y;                   Position of starting point in logical
                              coordinates
short boundary_color;         Color number of the boundary at which filling
                              should stop
```

Example Call

```
_floodfill(25, 75, 4);
```

Returns

The *_floodfill* function returns a nonzero value if the fill is successful. If there is an error, it returns a zero.

See Also

```
_setcolor, _setfillmask
```

__getcurrentposition ◄

Purpose

Use *_getcurrentposition* to obtain the logical coordinates of the current graphics position, which is maintained internally by the graphics library routines.

Syntax

```
#include <graph.h>
struct xycoord far _getcurrentposition(void);
```

Example Call

```
curpos = _getcurrentposition();
```

Returns

The *_getcurrentposition* function returns the logical coordinates of the current graphics position in an *xycoord* structure, which is described under *_getlogcoord*.

See Also

```
_moveto, _lineto
```

__getimage ◄

Purpose

Use the *_getimage* function to save a rectangular screen image in a buffer. You must allocate a sufficient amount of storage for the buffer and provide the buffer's address to *_getimage*.

Syntax

```
#include <graph.h>
```

```
void far _getimage(short x1, short y1, short x2, short y2,
                   char far *image_buffer);
short x1, y1;              Upper-left corner of rectangular boundary
                          of screen image to be saved
short x2, y2;             Lower-right corner of rectangular boundary
                          of screen image to be saved
char far *image_buffer;   Buffer where image is to be stored
```

Example Call

```
_getimage(50,50,100,100,image); /* Save the image */
```

See Also

_imagesize, _putimage

Example

Line 40 in Example 18-1 uses _getimage to save an image.

► **__getpixel**

Purpose

Use the _getpixel function to retrieve the pixel value of a specific pixel whose location is specified in logical coordinates.

Syntax

```
#include <graph.h>
short far _getpixel(short x, short y);
short x, y;    The logical x and y coordinates of the pixel whose value is
               returned
```

Example Call

```
pix_value = _getpixel(100, 150);
```

Returns

If the pixel is inside the clipping region, _getpixel returns the current pixel value. Otherwise, it returns −1 to indicate failure.

See Also

_setcliprgn, _setpixel, _setviewport

__getpixel

__imagesize ◄

Purpose

Use the _imagesize_ function to determine the number of bytes necessary to store a rectangular region of the screen. Call _imagesize_ before allocating memory to store an image or before storing the image with _getimage_.

Syntax

```
#include <graph.h>
long far _imagesize(short x1, short y1, short x2, short y2);
short x1, y1;    Upper-left corner of rectangular boundary of image
short x2, y2;    Lower-right corner of rectangular boundary of image
```

Example Call

```
bytes_needed = _imagesize(min_x, min_y, max_x, max_y);
```

Returns

The _imagesize_ function returns a long integer containing the number of bytes needed to store the specified rectangular screen image.

See Also

```
_getimage, _putimage
```

Example

Line 30 in Example 18-1 uses _imagesize_ to determine the buffer size necessary to hold a screen image.

__lineto, __moveto ◄

Purpose

Use _lineto_ to draw a line from the current position to a new point using the current color and the current line style. You can move to a new position by calling _moveto_. If you think in terms of drawing on a piece of paper with a pen, calling _moveto_ is analogous to lifting the pen and moving to a new point on the paper.

Syntax

```
#include <graph.h>
short far _lineto(short x, short y);
struct xycoord far _moveto(short x, short y);
short x, y;    Logical coordinates of point
```

Example Call

```
_moveto(10, 20);
_lineto(30, 50); /* Line from (10,20) to (30,50) */
```

Returns

The *_lineto* function returns a nonzero value if the line is drawn successfully. Otherwise, it returns a zero. The *_moveto* function returns the x and y coordinates of the previous graphics' position in a structure of type *xycoord* (see *_getlogcoord*).

See Also

```
_setcolor, _setlinestyle
```

Example

Example 18-2 uses *_lineto* and *_moveto* to plot *sin(x)* against *x*.

▶ **_pie**

Purpose

Use *_pie* to draw a filled or bordered pie-shaped wedge whose boundary consists of a segment of an ellipse and lines joining the center of the ellipse to the beginning and the end points of the segment. Figure 18-1 illustrates how to specify the shape of the *pie*.

Syntax

```
#include <graph.h>
short far _pie(short flag, short x1, short y1, short x2,
               short y2, short xb, short yb, short xe, short
                                                        ye);
```

short flag;	*Indicates whether to fill or just draw a border (Use constants from Table 18-2.)*
short x1, y1;	*Coordinates of upper-left corner of bounding rectangle of the ellipse to which the curved edge of the pie belongs*
short x2, y2;	*Coordinates of lower-right corner of bounding rectangle of the ellipse to which the curved edge of the pie belongs*
short xb, yb;	*The curved edge of the pie begins at the point where a line drawn from the center of the bounding rectangle to (xb, yb) cuts the ellipse*
short xe, ye;	*The curved edge of the pie ends at the point where a line drawn from the center of the bounding rectangle to (xe, ye) cuts the ellipse*

Example Call

```
_pie(_GFILLINTERIOR, 0, 150, 150, 200, 0, 150, 0, 200);
```

_pie

Returns

The return value is nonzero if everything goes well; otherwise, _pie returns a zero.

See Also

_setcolor, _setfillmask

_putimage ◄

Purpose

Use the _putimage function to display a rectangular screen image saved earlier by _getimage in a buffer. The manner in which the image is redrawn depends on the value of the short integer argument *action*. This argument should be one of the constants defined in the file *graph.h* and shown, along with their meanings, in Table 18-3.

Table 18-3. Interpreting the Action Constants for _putimage

Constants	Interpretation
_GAND	The image is drawn by performing a logical AND of the existing pixel value with the one from the saved image.
_GOR	The pixel values from the saved image are logically ORed with the existing pixel values in the area where the image is being drawn.
_GPRESET	Each bit in each pixel of the saved image is logically inverted, then these values are transferred to the screen, overwriting the existing image. Thus, for example, the areas of a saved EGA screen, which were yellow (pixel value 14 = 1110 in binary), will become blue (pixel value 1 = 0001 in binary).
_GPSET	The saved image is drawn at the specified area, completely overwriting any existing image.
_GXOR	Each pixel from the saved image is exclusive-ORed with the current pixels in the area where the image is being drawn. Very useful in animation because exclusive OR of an image with itself erases the image. Thus, the background can be restored easily with this action command.

Syntax

```
#include <graph.h>
void far _putimage(short x1, short y1, char far *image_buffer,
                   short action);
short x1, y1;              Logical coordinates of point on screen
                          where the upper-left corner of the
                          rectangular image will be placed
```

```
char far *image_buffer;        Buffer where image has been saved
short action;                  Command to _putimage instructing it to
                               redraw the saved image in a particular
                               manner
```

Example Call

```
_putimage(100, 200, image, _GXOR);
```

See Also

```
_imagesize, _getimage
```

Example

Example 18-1 uses _putimage to animate a small stick figure on the screen.

► __rectangle

Purpose

Use _rectangle to draw a filled or a bordered rectangle (See Figure 18-1.) Before calling _rectangle, use _setcolor to select the fill color, _setfillmask to select a fill pattern, and _setlinestyle to select a solid or a dashed line for the border.

Syntax

```
#include <graph.h>
short far _rectangle(short flag, short x1, short y1,
                                  short x2, short y2);
short flag;       To fill or to draw a border only (Use constants from Table
                  18-2.)
short x1, y1;     Coordinates of upper-left corner
short x2, y2;     Coordinates of lower-right corner
```

Example Call

```
_rectangle(_GBORDER, 100, 110, 250, 200);
```

Returns

The return value is nonzero if everything goes well. If there is an error, _rectangle returns zero.

See Also

```
_floodfill, _setcolor, _setfillmask, _setlinestyle
```

__rectangle

__setpixel ◀

Purpose

Use the _setpixel function to set a specific pixel to the current color. The location of the pixel is given in logical coordinates.

Syntax

```
#include <graph.h>
short far _setpixel(short x, short y);
short x, y;        The logical x and y coordinates of the pixel to be set to
                   current color
```

Example Call

```
_setpixel(120, 95);
```

Returns

If the pixel is inside the clipping region and _setpixel succeeds, it returns the previous pixel value. Otherwise, it returns −1 to indicate failure.

See Also

```
_getpixel, _setcliprgn, _setviewport
```

Example 18-1   Here is a program that uses _getimage and _putimage to animate a stick figure on the screen. The example is written assuming an EGA. Change the video mode to suit your system. (See Table 17-4 for a list of video modes.)

```
1:#include <stdio.h>
2:#include <malloc.h>
3:#include <graph.h>
4:#define YELLOW 14
5:main()
6:{
7:    char far *image;
8:    char buffer[80];
9:    short x=0, y=0;
10:    unsigned numbytes, c = 0;
11:/* Assume EGA. Put it in high-resolution graphics mode */
12:    if (_setvideomode(_ERESCOLOR) == 0)
13:    {
14:/* Error setting mode */
15:        printf("Not EGA hardware\n");
16:        exit(0);
17:    }
18:/* Draw a small stick figure to save */
19:    _setcolor(YELLOW);
```

```
20:    _ellipse(_GFILLINTERIOR,0,0,10,10);
21:    _moveto(5,10);
22:    _lineto(5,20);
23:    _lineto(0,30);
24:    _moveto(10,30);
25:    _lineto(5,20);
26:    _moveto(0,15);
27:    _lineto(0,10);
28:    _lineto(10,15);
29:/* Determine storage needed for the image */
30:    numbytes = (unsigned int)_imagesize(0,0,10,30);
31:/* Allocate buffer for image */
32:    if ((image = (char far *) malloc(numbytes)) ==
33:        (char far *)NULL)
34:    {
35:        _setvideomode(_DEFAULTMODE);
36:        printf(
37:             "Not enough memory for image storage\n");
38:        exit(0);
39:    }
40:    _getimage(x,y,10,30,image); /* Save the image */
41:
42:    _clearscreen(_GCLEARSCREEN);
43:    _settextposition(1,1);
44:    _outtext("Demonstrating animation with _putimage");
45:    _setlogorg(320,175);
46:    _putimage(x,y,image,_GXOR);
47:
48:/* Tell user how to use program and how to exit */
49:    _settextposition(24,1);
50:    _outtext("q = exit, h=left, j=down, k=up, l=right");
51:
52:/* Perform animation using _putimage */
53:    while(c != 'q')
54:    {
55:        c = getch();
56:/* First erase at last position */
57:        _putimage(x,y,image,_GXOR);
58:        switch(c)
59:        {
60:            case 'h': x -= 2; /* 2 pixels left */
61:                      break;
62:            case 'l': x += 2; /* 2 pixels right */
63:                      break;
64:            case 'j': y += 2; /* 2 pixels down */
65:                      break;
66:            case 'k': y -= 2; /* 2 pixels up   */
67:                      break;
68:        }
69:/* Redraw at new position */
70:        _putimage(x,y,image,_GXOR);
71:    }
```

```
72:/* Restore mode when done */
73:    _setvideomode(_DEFAULTMODE);
74:}
```

Example 18-2   The following program uses _moveto and
_lineto to draw a graph showing sin(x)
against x. The program assumes an EGA system.

```
 1:#include <stdio.h>
 2:#include <math.h>
 3:#include <graph.h>
 4:
 5:#define RED     4    /* Color number 4 is RED     */
 6:#define TWOPI  6.283 /* Approximate value of 2 Pi */
 7:#define MAXPNT 100   /* Points on the sinusoid    */
 8:
 9:main()
10:{
11:    struct videoconfig config;
12:    short i, x, y, oldx, oldy, midpoint;
13:    double xd, yd, ampl;
14:/* Enter hi-resolution graphics mode on EGA */
15:    if (_setvideomode(_ERESCOLOR) == 0)
16:    {
17:/* Error setting mode */
18:        printf("Mode not supported by hardware\n");
19:        exit(0);
20:    }
21:/* Get current configuration */
22:    _getvideoconfig(&config);
23:    midpoint = config.numypixels/2 - 1;
24:    ampl = (double)midpoint - 30.;
25:/* Let the logical origin be halfway down the screen */
26:    _setlogorg(0, midpoint);
27:/* Move to logical origin */
28:    _moveto(0,0);
29:    _settextposition(1,1);
30:    _outtext(
31:"Demonstrating _lineto with a plot of sin(x) vs x");
32:    _setcolor(RED);
33:
34:    for (i=0; i<=MAXPNT; i++)
35:    {
36:        yd = ampl *
37:            sin(TWOPI * ((double)i)/((double)MAXPNT));
38:        xd = ((double)config.numxpixels/2.0 - 1.)*
39:            (double)i / (double)MAXPNT;
40:        x  = (short)xd;
41:/* Negate y so that y axis is positive upwards    */
42:        y  = - (short)yd;
43:/* Draw a line to the new point by calling _lineto */
44:        _lineto(x,y);
```

```
45:    }
46:/* Restore original mode */
47:/* Give user a chance to see the result          */
48:   _settextposition(40,1);
49:   _outtext("Press any key to exit:");
50:   getch();
51:   _setvideomode(_DEFAULTMODE);
52:}
```

19

Combining Graphics and Text

Text is an essential part of graphics. For example, if you prepare a bar graph or a pie chart, you have to annotate the graph so that the user can understand the meaning of the plots. The Microsoft C graphics library includes seven routines to control text output in the graphics mode.

► __gettextcolor, __settextcolor

Purpose

Use the _*gettextcolor* function to get the value of the current text color parameter and _*settextcolor* to set a new value. The text color is a short integer value that is used as the attribute for each text character output by _*outtext*. Note that text printed by *printf* do not use these settings.

Syntax

```
#include <graph.h>
short far _gettextcolor(void);
short far _settextcolor(short color);
short color;       Text color to be set by _settextcolor
```

Example Call

```
txt_color_now = _gettextcolor();
old_txt_color = _settextcolor(4);
```

Returns

The _*gettextcolor* function returns a short integer containing the current value of the text color parameter, while _*settextcolor* returns its previous value.

Example

Line 19 in Example 19-1 uses _*settextcolor* to select a color for text output.

► __gettextposition, __settextposition

Purpose

Use _*gettextposition* to retrieve and _*settextposition* to set the current text position, which is where text output will appear if you call the output function _*outtext* or any other standard C output routine such as *printf*.

Syntax

```
#include <graph.h>
struct rccoord far _gettextposition(void);
struct rccoord far _settextposition(short row, short column);
short row, column;     Row and column relative to origin of text window
                       where new text output will begin
```

__gettextposition, __settextposition

Example Call

```
row_col_pos = _gettextposition();
old_pos = _settextposition(24, 1);
```

Returns

The *_gettextposition* function returns a *rccoord* structure, which contains the row and column defining the current "text position." The following structure is declared in the include file *graph.h*.

```
struct rccoord     /* Structure for text position    */
{
    short row;     /* row number of text position    */
    short col;     /* column number of text position */
};
```

See Also

```
_settextwindow
```

Example

Example 19-1 uses *_settextposition* to implement a data entry program.

__outtext ◄

Purpose

Use the *_outtext* function to display null-terminated C strings at the current text position (see *_settextposition*) using the current text color (see *_settextcolor*). To display formatted strings, first prepare output in a buffer (array of characters) by calling *sprintf*, then display the buffer by calling *_outtext* with the buffer address as the argument.

Syntax

```
#include <graph.h>
void far _outtext(char far *buffer);
char far *buffer;     Pointer to character buffer that holds the null-
                      terminated string to be printed by _outtext
```

Example Call

```
_outtext("Microsoft C Graphics");
```

See Also

```
_setactivepage, _settextcolor, _settextposition,
_settextwindow, _wrapon
```

Example

Lines 25 and 30 in Example 19-1 use *_outtext* for text output.

► __settextwindow

Purpose

Use *_settextwindow* to define a window for scrolled text output. The window is specified in terms of the row and column coordinates of its upper-left and lower-right corners. Similar windows for graphics can be defined by calling the *_setviewport* function.

Syntax

```
#include <graph.h>
void far _settextwindow(short r1, short c1, short r2, short
                                                         c2);
```

short r1, c1;	*Upper-left corner of text window in row and column coordinates*
short r2, c2;	*Lower-right corner of text window in row and column coordinates*

Example Call

```
_settextwindow(10, 10, 16, 70);
```

See Also

```
_clearscreen, _setbkcolor, _settextposition, _outtext
```

Example

Line 17 in Example 19-1 defines a text window by using *_settextwindow*.

► __wrapon

Purpose

Use the *_wrapon* function to control whether text being output by *_outtext* is clipped or wrapped onto the next line when the text string extends beyond the current text window. The default setting is to wrap long lines. The argument *flag* can take one of two defined values shown in Table 19-1. The interpretation of each value is also shown. These constants are defined in the include file *graph.h*.

__wrapon

Constant	Interpretation
_GWRAPOFF	Long lines are truncated at the edge of text window
_GWRAPON	Lines extending beyond the text window get wrapped onto a new line

Table 19-1. Constants Used by _wrapon

Syntax

```
#include <graph.h>
short far _wrapon(short flag);
short flag;      Turn wrapping on (_GWRAPON) or off (_GWRAPOFF)
```

Example Call

```
_wrapon(_GWRAPOFF);
```

Returns

The _wrapon function returns a short integer containing the value of the flag before the current call.

See Also

_outtext, _settextwindow

Example 19-1   The following is a data entry program written in Microsoft C. It uses _settextposition to position the cursor at the beginning of a field before accepting input for that field. You can implement data entry applications using this approach.

```
1:#include <graph.h>
2:#define RED      4L
3:#define YELLOW 14
4:#define ESC '\033'  /* ASCII code for the Esc key */
5:
6:static char *fieldlabel[4] =
7:{ "Name:", "Street:", "City/State/ZIP:", "Phone:"};
8:
9:static int fieldxy[4][2] = {3,16,4,16,5,16,6,16};
10:
11:main()
12:{
13:   int left=20, top=10, right=60, bottom=20,
14:       fieldnum = 0, maxfields = 4,
15:       numchar = 0, c, i;
16:/* Define a text window to be used as a form */
17:   _settextwindow(top,left,bottom,right);
18:   _setbkcolor(RED);
19:   _settextcolor(YELLOW);
20:   _clearscreen(_GWINDOW);
21:/* Let user fill the fields in the form. */
```

```
22:     _settextposition(1,10);
23:     _outtext("C L I E N T    D A T A");
24:     _settextposition(bottom-top,1);
25:     _outtext("<Enter> for next field. <Esc> to exit");
26:/* Mark the fields */
27:     for (i = 0; i < maxfields; i++)
28:     {
29:         _settextposition(fieldxy[i][0],1);
30:         _outtext(fieldlabel[i]);
31:     }
32:     _settextposition(fieldxy[fieldnum][0],
33:                     fieldxy[fieldnum][1]);
34:     while((c = getch()) != ESC)
35:     {
36:         if(c == '\r')
37:         {
38:/* Go to next field */
39:             fieldnum = (fieldnum+1) % maxfields;
40:             _settextposition(fieldxy[fieldnum][0],
41:                     fieldxy[fieldnum][1]);
42:             numchar = 0;
43:         }
44:         numchar++;
45:         if(numchar < (right - left
46:                 - fieldxy[fieldnum][1]))
47:         {
48:             if(c != '\r') putch(c);
49:         }
50:         else  putch('\a');
51:     }
52:}
```

Index

The Waite Group's Essential Guide to ANSI C

Naba Barkakati

An intermediate-level pocket guide for programmers, this book conforms to the American National Standards Institute's (ANSI) C draft and is the first book on the newly adopted standard for C. It provides a convenient and fast reference to all C functions, with examples for each, in a handy "shirt-pocket" size.

Topics covered include:

- How to Use This Essential Guide
- Overview of ANSI C
- The ANSI C Preprocess, Language, and Library
- Streams and Files in C
- ANSI C File Routine Reference
- Process Control
- Variable-length Argument Lists
- Memory Allocation and Management
- Data Conversion and Math Routines
- Character Classification and Conversion
- String Comparison and Manipulation
- Searching and Sorting
- Time Routines

224 Pages, 4¾ x 8½, Softbound
ISBN: 0-672-22673-1
No. 22673, $7.95

The Waite Group's Essential Guide to Turbo C®

Naba Barkakati

This user-friendly reference book explains all of the functions of the Turbo C library.

Compact and concise, the book covers all version 2.0 features including 8086 segments and offsets, paragraphs, code and data segments, heap, near and far data, and memory models.

Topics covered include:

- Overview of the Turbo C Language
- The Turbo C Programming Environment
- Process Control
- Variable Arguments
- Memory Allocation
- Buffer Manipulation
- Data Conversion
- Math Functions
- Character Classification and Conversion
- String Manipulation
- Searching and Sorting
- Time and Date Functions
- File and Directory Manipulation
- Input and Output Routines
- System Calls
- Graphics Modes, Coordinates, and Attributes
- Drawing and Animation
- Combining Graphics and Text
- Text Mode Routines

288 Pages, 4¾ x 8½, Softbound
ISBN: 0-672-22675-8
No. 22675, $7.95

Visit your local book retailer or call
800-428-SAMS.

The Waite Group's
C Primer Plus, Revised Edition

Mitchell Waite, Stephen Prata, and Donald Martin

This revised and expanded edition of a best-seller presents everything you should know to begin programming in the exciting C language, now used by over 80 percent of the software community.

Topics covered include:

■ Structure of a Simple C Program
■ Variables, Constants, and Data Types
■ Character Strings, # define, printf( ), and scanf( )
■ Operators, Expressions, and Statements
■ Input/Output Functions and Redirection
■ Choosing Alternatives: if, else, Relational and Conditional Operators
■ Storage Classes and Program Development
■ The C Preprocessor
■ Arrays and Pointers
■ Character Strings and String Functions
■ Structures and Other Data Delights
■ The C Library and File I/O
■ Bit Fiddling, Keywords, Binary Numbers, IBM® PC Music, and More

576 Pages, 7¹⁄₂ x 9³⁄₄, Softbound
ISBN: 0-672-22582-4
No. 22582, $24.95

Advanced C Primer ++

Stephen Prata, The Waite Group

Programmers, students, managers, and hackers alike, will learn to master the C programming language. Anyone who knows the basics of C will learn the practical C tips never before published. This indepth coverage gives you a rare and complete examination of video access ports, segmented memory, and registers.

Advanced C Primer + + takes the reader further than most C books on the market, showing how to manipulate the hardware of the IBM PC family of computers directly from C.

Topics covered include:

■ Advanced C Programming
■ Register and Bit Level System Control
■ Hardware Operation for Beginners and Experienced Users
■ Advanced Use of Pointers, Functions, Storage Classes, Arrays and Structures
■ C Library Access
■ Use of Assembly Language Modules
■ Binary and Text File Input and Output
Includes chapter questions and answers.

512 Pages, 7¹⁄₂ x 9³⁄₄, Softbound
ISBN: 0-672-22486-0
No. 22486, $24.95

Visit your local book retailer or call 800-428-SAMS.

Microsoft C Library Routines Arranged Alphabetically *(continued)*

getche, *193*
_getcolor, *237*
_getcurrentposition, *253*
getcwd, *158*
getenv, *49*
_getfillmask, *238*
_getimage, *253*
_getlinestyle, *239*
_getlogcoord, *240*
_getphyscoord, *240*
getpid, *50*
_getpixel, *254*
gets, *174*
_gettextcolor, *264*
_gettextposition, *264*
_getvideoconfig, *241*
getw, *174*
gmtime, *137*
goto, *18*
halloc, *70*
_harderr, *225*
_hardresume, *225*
_hardretn, *225*
heapchk, *66*
_heapset, *67*
_heapwalk, *67*
hfree, *71*
huge, *18*
hypot, *98*
if, *18*
_imagesize, *255*
inp, *194*
inpw, *194*
int, *19*
int86, *226*
int86x, *226*
intdos, *227*
intdosx, *227*
interrupt, *19*
isalnum, *106*
isalpha, *106*
isascii, *107*
isatty, *149*
iscntrl, *107*
isdigit, *107*
isgraph, *107*
islower, *107*
isprint, *107*
ispunct, *107*
isspace, *107*
isupper, *107*
isxdigit, *107*
itoa, *86*
j0, *99*

j1, *99*
jn, *99*
kbhit, *194*
labs, *90*
ldexp, *98*
ldiv, *95*
lfind, lsearch, *129*
_lineto, *255*
_loadds, *20*
localtime, *137*
locking, *150*
log, *99*
log10, *99*
long, *20*
longjmp, *50*
_lrotl, *100*
_lrotr, *100*
lseek, *188*
ltoa, *86*
_makepath, *151*
malloc, *68*
matherr, *101*
_memavl, *71*
memccpy, *76*
memchr, *76*
memcmp, *77*
memcpy, *76*
memicmp, *77*
_memmax, *71*
memmove, *78*
memset, *78*
mkdir, *158*
mktemp, *151*
mktime, *137*
modf, *101*
movedata, *79*
_moveto, *255*
_msize, *69*
near, *21*
_nfree, *65*
_nheapchk, *66*
_nheapset, *67*
_nheapwalk, *67*
_nmalloc, *68*
_nmsize, *69*
onexit, *46*
open, *189*
outp, *195*
outpw, *195*
_outtext, *265*
pascal, *21*
perror, *51*
_pie, *256*
pow, *102*
printf, *175*
putc, *178*
putch, *195*
putchar, *178*

putenv, *51*
_putimage, *257*
puts, *170*
putw, *174*
qsort, *129*
raise, *52*
rand, *102*
read, *191*
realloc, *72*
_rectangle, *258*
register, *21*
_remapallpalette, *243*
_remappalette, *243*
remove, *152*
rename, *152*
return, *22*
rewind, *178*
rmdir, *158*
rmtmp, *179*
_rotl, *100*
_rotr, *100*
_saveregs, *22*
sbrk, *73*
scanf, *179*
_searchenv, *159*
segread, *228*
_selectpalette, *243*
_setactivepage, *244*
_setbkcolor, *236*
setbuf, *181*
_setcliprgn, *245*
_setcolor, *237*
_setfillmask, *238*
setjmp, *52*
_setlinestyle, *239*
_setlogorg, *245*
setmode, *153*
_setpixel, *259*
_settextcolor, *264*
_settextposition, *264*
_settextwindow, *266*
setvbuf, *181*
_setvideomode, *246*
_setviewport, *245*
_setvisualpage, *244*
short, *22*
signal, *53*
signed, *23*
sin, *93*
sinh, *94*
sizeof, *23*
spawnl, *55*
spawnle, *55*
spawnlp, *55*
spawnlpe, *55*